Instant Country, Just Add People!

*Niihau * Lanai * Kahoolawe * UEIR*

Instant Country, Just Add People!

*Niihau * Lanai * Kahoolawe * UEIR*

Horus Michael

Instant Country, Just Add People!

Copyright © ® 2017 Horus Michael,

All Rights Reserved.

No part of this publication may be reproduced or transmitted in any form or by any means, electronic or mechanical, including photocopying, recording or any other information storage and retrieval system, without prior permission in writing from the Author or Copyright holder. Reviewers may quote brief passages.

This book was printed in the **United States of America**. **This book is a product of the Kingdom of Niihau, UEIR.**

10 9 8 7 6 5 4 3 2 1

www.amazon.com/author/horusmichael

Photos © MS Word Clip Art & © Author (M7).

Genre: Political Science, Utopia.

"The Fate of One-Star Reviewers"

Contents:

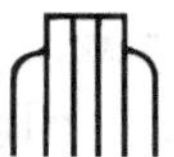

Each Citizen will be recorded by the State. The State will have a **DNA Genetic Database on all Citizens** for identity purposes, and to track criminals entering or leaving the country. The Department of Health will advise Citizens using their DNA samples, as obtained by the mouth using cheek cells or blood sample. Each Citizen will have their **PIN** or Personal Identification Number encoded on all passports, licenses, or health care documents. Their **Banking** information will be connected to this PIN number, so the State has **correct information for Tax purposes** only. This will eliminate the need for Tax preparation or asking how much tax one owes the State. Citizens can still keep their money in **cash form** or other financial institutions, such as Time Banks or Barternotes.

Anyone **who steals** another's identity will not be able to verify their identity once Genetic sampling occurs. The PIN number is on **Citizen Universal Passes**, which acts as a passport to all developed Nations and for basic identity in the country.

Drugs used as **pain medicine** which is illegally produced and sold by criminals, will be legalized to remove the criminal element and regulated by the State for **revenue**. **Recreational usage** will be allowed in sealed hotel-styled buildings away from Citizens, with entrance fees or a subscription. Citizens who use these drugs must be **completely sober upon leaving** the sealed buildings with a required Health Examination.

Homelessness will **not** be a crime. **Public facilities will be constructed and enforced by paid or volunteer employment**, such as Free Health Care, Bath houses, Hotels, Thrift Stores, Libraries and Museums, Schools or Distant-learning Colleges, and Job placement in this system.

Companies may be owned by the State **for revenue**, with tax-exemption of its employees and CEO. All other companies are taxed at a **minimum of 3%** to a maximum of 15% monthly income as revenue to the State, **except for** non-income earning or "volunteer" non-profit companies. When the economy improves this amount **is reduced**.

Violent criminals such as Gangs or religious or political extremists will be given to work for the Military to test products, in place of prison. **Non-violent criminals** such as driving violations, tax evasion, sex crimes, or technology related crimes will work for the **Department of Rehabilitation**, not to prison. Prisons will exist **only** for POWs (Prisoners of War), spies, police who commit crimes against Citizens, and the like. This should **reduce tax burdens** for the country. As all Citizens have DNA recorded, the prisoners or criminals cannot "go anywhere."

Citizen Tax rate is 10% Monthly taxable income, **or** up to 30% Annual taxable income; these are **only maximums** allowed by Law, and **may be reduced** when the economy is strong or without debts. Minimum is 1% Monthly income per Citizen above age 17, **except** child prodigies who graduate college early.

Taxable Income: gifts above minimum threshold amount (In 2017, it is $2000+ USD per month), salaries, book or music royalties, sales of new products (not used products), sales from recycled materials, technology stocks, Energy sales (includes solar or wind surpluses), gambling income higher than played with, products, services, farming, Art, Science surplus or research, etc.

State Lotteries: only taxable amount is 5% of winnings from Annuity, or 10% of lump sum winnings. Tips or donations are considered gifts. Elders above age 55, unemployed, handicapped or disabled, non-prodigy children under the age of 19 years, College students, hospitalized or institutionalized Citizens, **Pharaohs** and their Courts, Temples, Military Veterans, and non-profit groups are **exempt** from normal taxes. **Non-Citizens** may be subject to Taxes after 1 month of residency.

Unused revenue will be **recycled** to pay debts, kept in the Treasury until needed, or paid for reconstruction of domestic cities following any Natural Disaster or other event.

Education will limit exposure to unrelated information or knowledge, except for extra credit papers. This will reduce crime and prevent individuals from joining extremist political, technological or religious groups like terrorists or other groups. This includes propaganda videos to recruit criminals or terrorists (as in 2017 CE). The Internet access will be regulated for anyone under the Age of Reason and Responsibility. This is for their protection.

Foreign nations who require Aid are subject to State compensation following such Aid, from 5% to 10% value of said Aid, after it is successful in the Nation; whoever asks our Government for Economic, Political, Military, Religious/Magical or Civil Assistance **is indebted unto us at least one month afterwards.** This debt may be used to reduce any Trade Tariffs or act as **credit** with any trade coming from them. This aid includes Divine Intervention.

Farms are to be owned or regulated by the State, and may exist inside large Greenhouses, multi-level buildings in place of land when such land is scarce. These interior farms are powered by solar or wind energy to power sun lamps and irrigation, etc. Wells or water towers shall supply local water. Recycled water from sanitation may also be helpful in this. Farm animals shall be well-treated and their products **not priced higher** than any other product.

If a space station or Lunar/Planetary Base is acceptable, **asteroid mining** will supply the State for minerals. 40% of asteroid mining revenue will go to the Department of Travel, Immigration, and Space Exploration. The other 60% will be individual revenue only.

Citizens are responsible for their own actions, and the State will **not** be required to defend them when Citizens act on their own **to attack a foreign nation**, or express "delusions of Freedom." **Freedom is the absence of Laws and Order**. America started out as a Penal Colony enslavement from the British Empire. So they wanted Freedom from the British King. The British invaded America to regain their **serfs**, but saw that the Native Population was "larger" so they fled and the colonists claimed victory and founded their own country, the USA. Over time the Native Population died from European biological illnesses that they had no immunity for. The First American President, George Washington, was a **Freemason**. The Freemasons or Masons are descended from the Ancient Egyptian architects and artisans of Pharaoh; they designed the USA to eventually connect to the **UEIR**. **The Great Seal of the USA** shows the Pyramid of Khufu with the Sun glinting off the gold plated capstone on one side, with the other side showing the Falcon god **Horus** "Eagle" with the Solar crown above his head, when one connects the dots/stars to form a star. The 13 colonies are like the 12 Signs of the Zodiac with **Ra** the Sun at the center, or Christ at the Last Meal.

The Pledge of Allegiance to the Flag of USA is of Ancient Egyptian origin, but was around while Napoleon I was excavating Egypt. **Placing one's hand over the heart is a "salute to Ra" and the Flag is a hieroglyph for Deity.** So you are actually worshiping Ra the Sun God of Ancient Egypt, "One Nation under Ra." Egypt was the "Two Lands united by Pharaoh," and USA is 50+ Lands united together.

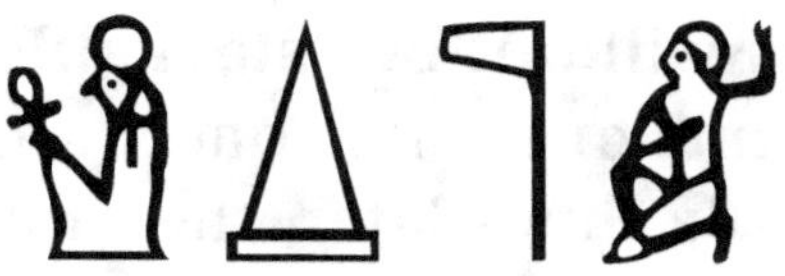

Citizens who can use **Egyptian Magic** for "Psychic/Magical Warfare" will assist the Military against any opposition or political enemies of the State. **Literacy** is important for this as Egyptian Magic **currently exists** in Magic Spell books. The Spells incorporate ideas from Egyptian Polytheist Names (*i.e. Deity Names when read or invoked cause events*).

Military training: [Required]: Mastery of Defensive and Offensive (& Weapons training) **Martial Arts**, *The Art of War* by Sun Tzu, Survival training, First Aid, Technology training, **with optional** Military or Cultural History. This occurs in a Military College. *Mercenaries are optional.*

Drones, AI, and machines may eventually replace ground troops and other human soldiers, with **technicians** as a solution. The UEIR shall build or retain a "Drone Factory" to build this new army. Drones will carry a mini-factory to create smaller Drones in a Military Zone. These can help as spies, explosive devices, targeted assassination, weather forecast, or other uses.

Crimes will not be "stackable" – when a person commits one crime once, then the same crime 10x times later, the first crime will count and the other 10x will **not require** separate Court trials. Numeration may input a number for punishment such as 10x instances of flogging or public humiliation per crime committed.

Laws may be edited in description when necessary *("Loitering = Lollygagging"; i.e. Wandering)*, and may not exist as a Vendetta against a person or group, and Over-legislation (*too many laws limiting Freedoms*) will be illegal. Over Punishment for one crime or "Stacked crimes" is also illegal; so no "life sentence plus 300 years in prison." **Laws must be written with Ma'at** (*Egyptian Legal Philosophy*).

The **State Budget** will be in percentages of **10%** per subject category. **Military** will be listed as "Security." **Infrastructure** contains roads and bridges, retaining walls and aqueducts, airports and seaports, warehouses, cemeteries, environmental conditions, weather stations, homeless shelters, bomb shelters or Natural Disaster storage and shelters, farms, satellites, and weapon deterrents. **Education** is schools (**K-12**), colleges and universities, art, libraries and museums, Egyptian Temples, research groups, technology and medical research, technology upgrades, archaeology and history groups, Space Exploration, and the Internet. **Health** is First Aid, hospitals and clinics, drug companies (Pharmaceutical), rehabilitation, Mental Health, Contraception, Disease Prevention, clean water and air, Welfare, Social Security, trauma centers, Genetic Modification (Medical Farms), and Medical Colleges. **Energy** is Natural Resources, solar/wind/oil/hybrid/coal/etc. **Political** is for Government Employees salaries, protection, and legislation. **Security** (**Military**) is for soldiers, drones, automatons, vehicles, technology, training, defense, police and Law Enforcement, Judges and Juries, protection, armor and weapons, ammunition, and Counter Intelligence/Counter Terrorism.

Estimated Budget:

The **Treasury** receives 10% of each <u>Budget</u> as **savings**.

Military-Security: 10%

Infrastructure: 10%

Education: 10%

Health: 10%

Energy: 10%

Political: 10%

Treasury: 10% (saved)

Monuments: 10% (Pyramids, Obelisks)

Entertainment: 5%

Pharaoh's expenses: 5%

Housing/sanitation/recycling: 5%

Territory Expansion (Real Estate): 5%

Sanitation includes Environmental protection, and overall cleanliness. Solid waste may be converted into fertilizer for farming or gardens. Recycled materials may be exported to factories or used by the local population as raw materials.

Chapter 2: Pharaoh's Education

To be a Pharaoh, study the following subjects *thoroughly*:

World History, Roman & Egyptian History, Chronology, Babylonian Laws (*Hammurabi*), Roman Philosophy (*Tacitus, Ovid, Cicero, Caesar, Marcus Aurelius*), Egyptian Religion & Magic systems, Encyclopedia of Military History (*from Thutmose 3 to Napoleon I*), Egyptian Architecture, Geography, Archaeology, Cultural Anthropology, Numerology, Geometry, Languages, Art, Fiction Writing or Literature, Egyptian Philosophy (*Ptah-hotep, Amonhotep son of Hapu, Wenis, Imhotep*), Ma'at Concept, Archery, Martial Arts, the Art of War (*Sun Tzu*), Agriculture, Ethics, Social Etiquette, Computer Programming, Diplomacy, Telepathy, Social Organization, Meditation, and Leadership.

The UEIR Senate is comprised of Senators **whom advise the Pharaoh**. Senators draft Legislation for the people whom they serve and send it to Pharaoh to approve or reject. Pharaoh may also write Legislation as necessary in his/her spare time and as **Edicts** (*Temporary Laws*).

Senators are not elected officials. To be a Senator you must first become a King, and *then retire* to the Senate. Senators serve as the official word of Pharaoh, in the method of the Ennead or *9 Sovereign Princes of Atlantis*. This usually happens when a King cannot renew his or her reign following the **Jubilee Festival** held *every* **15 to 30 years**. The Festival determines fitness to remain King as with a simple race around a track or other simple and intelligent exam. This is the equivalent of "Term Limits."

The Priesthood – the High Priests of AmonRa or Ptah – **advises the Pharaoh** on morally pressing issues. The **Viceroy** or Military Advisor also influences the Pharaoh.

Legislation must adhere to the concept of Ma'at and be **clear and concise** without confusion or preference. No loopholes are allowed. No lawyer games are allowed. No vendetta laws are allowed. *Justice is the vengeance of the victim over the aggressor.* We just use Courts to enforce it. Magic can enforce Ma'at on the sublime level. Magic is the will of Pharaoh, the medium between Earth and Duat. Laws are not made like Swiss cheese – no holes are in them. **An Elder Council** judges the people in lower Courts, while Pharaoh oversees higher Courts.

Kings (**Pharaoh**) may occupy one State or foreign Province each. The central Kings are called Pharaoh; the foreign or distant Kings are called **Sultan**. The religious King is the *Caliph*, or Successor. A co-regent King is a Prince.

Each **Citizen** is a Citizen-Soldier *when* enforcing the will of the people with Egyptian Magic. **Each Citizen has the capacity to become Pharaoh.** If a Citizen studies all listed subjects and excels in Egyptian Magic, the Citizen *can become a Pharaoh* in unoccupied positions or serve as a replacement when needed (following Jubilee Festival).

In place of **royal hunting grounds** for entertainment the Pharaoh may play computer games. This includes Virtual Reality sports.

Egyptian Temples are like Libraries, Colleges, Museums, Courts, religious shrines, storage, and Palaces. Online or Virtual Temples as websites work too.

Pharaohs may entertain entities from Duat when needed. *Or they may reign in Duat.* The **UEIR** is based in the Egyptian Netherworld of Duat, so it shall still be there by the time you exit Earth. Former Earthly Pharaohs are UEIR Senators. Senators may appoint the next Pharaoh, if desired.

Other offices such as **Nomarchs** (from county magistrates who govern "Nomes") and **Viceroys** may be elected by Full Citizens or appointed by Pharaoh or the Senate. **If no heir** to Pharaoh is available, the selection will be a lottery from **Full Citizens** who are qualified. The remainder of the monetary value of the **lottery** shall pay the expenses of Pharaoh. The lottery shall be random as from a computer device that drops numbered balls into a cauldron to select the Citizen (as with modern Lotteries or Inter-State Lotteries in USA, in 2017 CE).

Political Election Parties or Groups shall use names from Egyptian Deities (list), such as "Ra", "Sobek", "Set," "Horus", "Hathor," etc. The group shall incorporate divine attributes to the basis of that name. So "Ra" group shall include "solar energy", "Majesty", "Justice", or other attributes to the Group's social identity or purpose.

Elections shall imitate the Unification of Egypt by Horus Narmer in the process, **if televised.** Mock "election battles" between candidates shall imitate the battles of Horus vs. Seth for formation of Pharaoh, to bring honor to **Lord Osiris**.

Election candidates must be educated and literate, though a College degree is desired but not required of all candidates due to age. College degrees may be attained during the reign of Pharaoh should s/he be under-aged. Candidates must complete a Physical (Medical) exam prior to becoming Pharaoh. Pharaoh may appoint a successor **if** the successor meets the **necessary** qualifications.

Health Care is **not discriminatory** towards health conditions or "pre-existing conditions." Health Care is open to all Citizens, and non-citizens as with Emergency rooms; non-citizens will be billed for the services rendered after 1 month of residency. This includes prevention of epidemics (etc.). **Medical drugs** must be **tested** prior to use (*on violent criminals*) to oversee side-effects and future medicines. **Medical waste** should be disposed of in such a way as to not become dangerous or pollutant. Clean recycling is also an option.

State Bureaucracy (Scribes) is covered under Education or Political. This is for recording information, records, paperwork, offices, Copyrights, Patents, Titles, Citizen documents, and Taxes.

Chapter 3: Economy

In previous Egyptian regimes, Food was the **currency** of the State. Food was grown along the Nile and stored in granaries, found in houses and also in State Temples (Grain Banks), which were debited when needed. The people were paid for labor with food. They were not "slaves" as the Hebrews believed. The Hebrews later misinformed the Romans and other cultures about this. The workers, when not farming, **built monuments** during Flood Season, to prevent idleness or crime from unemployment. Prisoners did not stay in prisons; they were put to work. Some prisoners of war were educated and returned home, so they knew about the country who they invaded.   Obesity was seen as "prosperity." Carbohydrate diets of "bread and beer" will cause obesity.

Egyptian religion was based on their **Science**. In Ancient Egyptian religion, the Sun revolved around the Earth. It descended underground at night and fought demons until it rose up victoriously at dawn. The people were also kept in the dark about Eclipses. They feared unless they did something the Sun would never return from the darkness.

Egyptian religion was also very **materialistic.** They built statues like Ushabtis for the tombs (*Ushabtis represented personal servants for the Afterlife*), amulets of semi-precious stones, gold, and other materials. They made gold and silver bowls, spoons, ewers and other wares. Tombs, mummies, trinkets, fine linen wrappings, grave goods, and the like were all from **Osiris worship** and the belief in the Afterlife. So the religion helped shape the **Economy.** Today we do the same with popular stories, **movies**, films, computer games, etc. Today we have toys and action-figures of actors, glassware with film logos, trinkets, books and DVDs, etc.

Currency *may exist as* units of Labor, recorded by the Time it takes to work; this is called Time Currency. **Time Currency** is recorded on a ledger in a Time Bank, but also may be printed as paper money. Time Currency is a **substitute** for other paper money such as US Dollars, which are based on the state of the Economy, such as the Stock Market performance, popularity of its Government, stability of the country, and other factors.

The currency of the UEIR has many facets or types. There is the National Currency and a Popular Currency.

The **National Currency** is the **CAESAR**. Caesars are basically recycled gold and silver. *The set value is based on happiness of the Citizens.* The **Popular Currency** is the **Barternote.** This is maintained by the People, and may have a value based on factors such as Fame, attraction, artistic expression, knowledge, trade, literary expression, fashion, etc. **Other currencies** are in the individual Provinces or separate Kingdoms. For example, in the ***Province of Iapana*** is the Barternote of the Technocracy of Iapana (Stock value of the Government). In the ***Kingdom of Ni'ihau*** is the **Kahelelani**, based on the value of the shell of that name. Both appear as paper money in postcards or business cards format.

The old **Prophecy** that said **Lord Osiris returns to Earth** and reestablishes an Egyptian State is fulfilled once the great evil is vanquished. In my prophetic novel (*Eye of the Pharaoh ©1990-1995 MC*) I wrote the war on Arabic Terrorists would cease and the **UEIR** would be founded afterwards. This worked for in 2014 the evil Caliphate was created, and once it is destroyed the UEIR will rise up in its place. This Prophecy **was usurped by** the Christian religion for the Return of Christ and foundation of the Kingdom of God (Osiris).

The **UEIR Economy** is currently based on the **assets owned by Pharaoh M7** in USA (which are **currently secret** since M7 was classified by the CIA.) These **assets** were once **leaked** to the Public. This includes a *"Hotel, Tech business, museum, 2+ islands, Egyptian Temple or Library, and other businesses on the islands."* The **owed Revenue** will pay the expenses for the State and Government, including any *classified* income. The UEIR Tax Code from 1999 Code Caesar is **amended** by this book. The 1996 Plebeian Law Code has since been revoked as it was temporary. The USA has marketed the UEIR since 1993.

Other economic factors are M7's personal "books/novels" economy which does **not affect** the Government in terms of revenue.

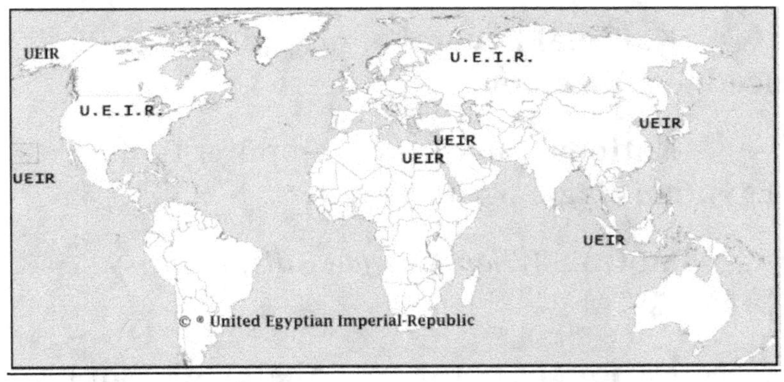

UEIR © M7 2017

Chapter 4: The Kingdom of Ni'ihau

Government type: Pharaocracy

National Anthem: Conch Shell (1.5 Minutes exhale)

National Religion: Pharaohism

Ruler: Pharaoh (1), Council of Viziers; One Vizier per State; non-State Provinces have Consuls. The Vizierate is a Senate of Viziers.

Laws: Code Maat (*Code Caesar series*).

National Animal: Blue Whale (or Monk Seal)

National Flower: White Lotus flower or Plumeria.

National Beverage: Arnold Palmer (½ Iced tea, ½ Lemonade)

National Pastimes: Computer Games, Egyptian Magic, write novels.

Motto: *"When Science fails, Fantasy prevails."*

National Currency: Kahelelani (Kah.); 1 Kah= $1000 USD. Currency is finite, and can be traded or cashed in for shells when available.

Taxes: **10% or Tithe** of Population per 2 Month Interval; unless exempted (Ex: disabled, elderly, Pharaoh, Veteran, etc.). **Sales Tax is 5%.** Nationalized (Government owned) businesses allow for less personal taxes.

Debts: If debts are **not paid** in 3 Years' Time the debt is voided by Law and the Credit Rating is lowered by 0.01% each time as incentive to pay debts on time (This is called *The Debt-Tender Law*).

Military Conscription: **Psychic Warfare** soldiers are recruited once they are proven to have an ability worth exploiting; age 17+ to 55 years of age. They need **not** be sent to a foreign country and can work here.

Psychic Warfare Soldiers should read the book, "*Effective Egyptian Magic Spells* © *Horus Michael, 2014*" or its equivalent.

Taxes pay for the Pharaocracy (Pharaoh & his Court, Palaces, general maintenance, insignia, servants, Temples & Priesthood, etc.), the Viziers (law makers and enforcers), the Imperial Treasury (savings, & bank), real estate owned by Pharaoh, and the Imperial Guard. Once that is complete, the funds go to a General Fund Pool or the Imperial Treasury and other Temple "Granaries."

Tax Exemptions:

Pharaoh & His Court (The Pharaocracy), Viziers, the Vizierate, Viceroys of the Military (our word for General of the Army or representative of the Military), Temples & Priests, Akua / Neteru incarnate or visible, Veterans of the Military or Foreign Dignitaries, Disabled people, the Elderly, people with fixed incomes or listed as Poor (below 30 Kah per year, or $30,000 USD), non-resident Alii, homeless people, criminals in prison, children, pets, Natives of Niihau, and the like **are Exempt from Income Taxes.**

Taxes may be paid by: Bank Check, Niihau Shells, Kahelelani Currency, Barter, Precious Metals or Stones, Paycheck deductions, Real Estate acquisitions, Company Products (from Companies), Services Credit, unopened packaged Food & Drink/Clothing/ textiles, labor, Time Credits (Time Dollars); favors, cooperation, good will, obedience, etc.

Physical Tax revenue may be paid by Bank Check, Cash, Precious Metals/Stones, Service Credits, book royalties, or IRS Refunds.

Income Taxes are to be collected or sent bi-monthly or **at least twice per year** (Solstices).   Niihau entrance fee is $100 per person, per day (*unless Exempt*).

(Law) Code of Maat (*Code Caesar Series*)

Introduction:

The **Code Caesar** is the Official Provincial Civil Code for **the UEIR** on Earth. It is named after *Gaius Julius Caesar*, the original designer or **Founder of the UEIR** (and would have been official if the *Ides of March* event never happened), & *Osiris, the First King*.

Each Province constitutes an annexed land or conquered vassal of the UEIR, and is governed by a Consul or King. One must be at least some form of King or its equivalent to serve as a Senator in the Imperial Senate. This is the *Kingdom of God* in the Osirian (later, Christian) prophecy.

UEIR Laws are enforced by **Angels** and other spiritual beings. Each Citizen is assigned a Guardian Angel (**Akhu**) to protect and guide him or her. These are summonable from Duat. UEIR Laws are also enforced by Psychic Commands or "Magic" / "Heka." Kheri-Heb Priests, Kahuna Priests, etc. can give orders to Angels for enforcement.

Punishment for violations can exist on Earth or in Duat; negative events are common (fires, accidents, Natural Disasters/Acts of God, floods, quakes, tsunamis, economic factors/recessions, etc.). A permanent punishment can take the form of a curse or jinx, until dispelled by an Official of Government (UEIR). Each level is numerical, and begins with one level, and can escalate due to severity of crime.

Crimes and Levels of Punishment:

1. **Warning.** Given as a Citation for an accident, infraction, disturbance of Peace, or premeditation of a crime without action.
2. **Minor.** Low level Crime that incurs a Fine; can be paid with money, barter exchange, labor, Time Credits, Community Service, other compensation, and multiplies in amount by 10% in coin per count of future crimes.
3. **Major.** High level Crime that incurs a Heavy Fine, unpaid labor (construction of monuments, buildings, or mental layout if physical disability is present), Community Service (one month per crime), Deprogramming Sessions in a Mental Facility (for violent crimes or multiple theft crimes), medication, branding with Bar Code for Tracking Purposes (if imprisoned by foreign nation or released), Limited Removal of Citizen (or Plebe) Rights, etc.
4. **Permanent.** Top Level Crime that incurs 150% of a Heavy Fine, Natural Disaster, exile, Divine Execution and transference to Duat for Judgment, banishment, the equivalent of Life in Prison (USA), and removal of Citizen Rights for duration decided by Courts; or physical / mental punishment(s).

A Standard English Dictionary may be required for interpretation of these Laws:

List of Violations with Number of level:

STEALING:

Armed robbery: 3

Normal, unarmed robbery: 2

Theft of items: 2

Theft of Valuables: 2, 3

Theft of Food in a Store: 1, 2

Shoplifting: 2

Major Shoplifting: 3

Copyright Infringement: 2, 3

Plagiarism (unpaid, Cultural): 2

Plagiarism (paid): 2, 3

Mugging (on a public street): 2, 3

Kidnapping (people): 3

Kidnapping (animal): 2, 3

Computer or Internet theft: 2

File Sharing (paid): 2

In Computer Game (online): 1, 2

Embezzlement (paid): 3

Conspiracy to Steal: 2, 3

Patent Theft: 2, 3

Piracy, (software, film, real or online): 2, 3

Computer Hacking: 2, 3

STEALING:

Stealing Personal Data (Identity theft): 2, 3

Data Mining or Phishing: 2, 3

Crookedness: 2, 3

Price Gouging, Petty Theft: 2, 3

Market Manipulation: 2, 3

Deceptive Advertising: 2, 3

Deceiving Elderly or Disabled: 3

Obtaining Classified Data: 3

Other Computer Theft: 2, 3

Computer Viruses (use): 3

Key loggers: 3

Key Duplication (non-owner): 2, 3

Cloning (non-medical): 2, 3

Conquering (non-UEIR): 3

From Temples, Churches: 2, 3

From (Education) Facilities: 2, 3

From States: 2, 3

From Pharaoh: 3

False Advertising: 2, 3

Mail Fraud, Bank Fraud: 2, 3

False Business: 2, 3

Con Artistry (paid): 3

Entrapment: 3

STEALING:

Eavesdropping (non-personal): 2

Wire-Tapping (Personal): 2, 3

Espionage (non-UEIR): 3

Agricultural Theft: 2, 3

Artifact Theft: 3

Hoarding (paid): 2, 3

Photocopying (non-personal): 1, 2

Forgery of Currency: 3

Forgery of Artifacts: 3

Forgery of UEIR Government: 3

False Claims: 2, 3

False Inheritance Claims: 2, 3

False Charity: 2, 3

Unofficial Marketing: 2, 3

Grand Theft: 2, 3

Hidden Fees: 2, 3

Immoral Company TOS: 3

Waiving Personal Rights: 2, 3

Undisclosed Fees: 2, 3

Fake/Lead Coins (not gold): 2, 3

Money Laundering, *Ponzi* scheme: 2, 3

Pyramid Scheme, Scams: 2, 3

Other Stealing: 2, 3

KILLING:

Abortion (multiple, Late Term): 2, 3

Abortion (inconvenience): 2, 3

Abortion (non-genetic defect): 2, 3

Premeditated, multiple (Serial Killing): 3

Mass Murder, Genocide: 3, 4

Murder-Suicide: 3, 4

Attempted Murder-Suicide: 3

Terrorism with Murder: 3, 4

Terrorism with Malice: 3

Terrorism with Destruction: 3

Assault with Weapons: 2, 3

Assault with Intent to Kill: 3

Unintentional Assault: 2, 3

Accidental Assault with Weapon: 1, 2

Accidental Assault: 1, 2

Accidental Killing (person): 2

Accidental Killing (other): 2

Driving with Intent: 3

Driving Accidental Death: 2

Driving with Distraction: 2, 3

DUI (alcohol or drugs): 2, 3

DUI with Internet: 2, 3

DUI (multiple): 3

KILLING:

Cannibalism (human): 3

Sports Killing (Endangered Species): 2, 3

Hunting (non-Food; non-Niihau): 2

Technology Abuse (animals): 2, 3

Chemical use (on people): 2, 3

Killing with Big Weapons (WMD): 3

Nuclear War: 3, 4

Deity Impersonation: 2, 3

Rioting: 2, 3

Military Incursion: 3

Protesting (armed): 3

Protesting (peaceful): 1, 2

Subversion: 3

Peaceful Terrorism: 2

Anarchy, Supporting Hostility: 3

Religious Terrorism: 2

Destruction of Property: 2, 3

Vandalism, Effacement: 2, 3

Destroying Monuments: 3, 4

Extremism with Violence: 3

Paid Assassination: 3, 4

Assassination: 3, 4

Conspiracy to Kill: 3

KILLING:

Attempting to overthrow Government: 3

Killing Ecosystem: 2, 3

Medical Testing Abuse (animals): 2, 3

Food Procurement Abuse (animals): 3

Animal Abuse: 2, 3

Human Abuse: 2, 3

Other Abuse: 2, 3

Elderly Abuse & Neglect: 2, 3

Assisted Suicide: 2, 3

Attempted Suicide or Murder: 2, 3

Suicide (as a Weapon): 3, 4

Forced Suicide: 3

Drug use that kills: 2, 3

Medical Malpractice: 3

Dental Malpractice: 2, 3

Single Murder: 3

Manslaughter (unintended Killing): 2, 3

Internet Hoax that results in Death: 3

Killing Police or Government (UEIR): 3

Assaulting Police or Government (UEIR): 2, 3

Poisoning: 2, 3

Causing Diseases: 2, 3

Other Killing: 2, 3

DECEPTION:

Lying under Oath: 2, 3

Lying to God(s), (Akua): 3

Lying to Goddess(es): 3

Lying to Angels: 2, 3

Deceptive Behavior: 2

Forged Documents, Autograph: 2, 3

Forgeries in General: 2, 3

Deception of TOS: 3

Un-disclosure of Facts: 2, 3

Deceptive Marketing: 2, 3

Deceptive Documentation: 2, 3

Industrial (Domestic) Espionage: 3

Lying in Court, to Government: 2, 3

Political Deception: 3

Contract Deception: 2, 3

Terms of Service Deception: 2, 3

Stealing Passwords, Impersonation: 3

Identity Theft: 3

Overall Crookedness: 3

Corruption (bribery, extortion): 2, 3

General Conspiracy: 3

Greed; Envy, Wrath, Sloth, Lust, etc.: 2, 3

Deliberate "Stupidity": 1, 2

DECEPTION:

Bringing False Witness(es): 3

False Pedigree, Education: 2, 3

False Rank (Military, Police): 2, 3

Dressing as Government (UEIR): 2, 3

Using Same Insignia as UEIR (M7): 3

False Pretending: 2

False Imprisonment (by Foreign Police, etc.): 2

False Valor (UEIR): 2

False Inheritance: 2, 3

Political Incorrectness: 2

Forgery of (Niihau) Shells: 3

Forgery of Precious Metals, items: 3

Copyright Deception: 3

Patent Deception: 2, 3

Immoral Gossip: 2, 3

(With Perjury) Slander or Libel: 3

Malicious Rumors, Misinformation: 2, 3

Making People Cry from Deception: 2

Deceptive Terrorism: 2, 3

Disrespect (of Citizens, UEIR): 2

Deceptive Quality of Products: 2, 3

Other Deception: 2, 3

DESTRUCTION:

Assault, multiple: 2, 3

Assault, single: 2

Assault, mental: 2

Assault, minor (slap): 2

Assault with Weapon: 2, 3

Assault with training: 2, 3

Assault, military: 3

General Violence: 2

Vandalism, Graffiti: 2, 3

Monument Destruction, effacement: 3

Religious element: 2, 3

Religious Extremist: 2, 3

Terrorism, destruction: 3

Explosives (non-military): 2, 3

Illegal Fireworks: 2, 3

IED Device: 3

Booby-trap: 2, 3

Snare, Trip Wire: 2, 3

Grenade (non-UEIR): 2, 3

Bombs on Vehicle: 3

Laser Weapons, (Non-UEIR): 3

Chemical, Nuclear Weapons: 3

Biological Weapons: 3

DESTRUCTION:

Psychic Weapons (Non-UEIR): 3

Psychic War (Non-UEIR): 3, 4

General War (non-UEIR): 3

War Crimes (non-UEIR): 3, 4

Crimes against God(s): 3, 4

Crimes against Earth: 3

Crimes against Humanity (Chaos): 2, 3

Crimes against Nature: 3

Vehicle Destruction: 2, 3

Private Property Damage: 2, 3

Sign Post Damage: 2

Infrastructure Damage: 2

Poisoning Water System, Salting Farms: 3

Exploding a Device: 3

Airplane bombings: 3, 4

Transportation Terrorism: 3, 4

Animal Provocation, bites: 2, 3

Torture (non-UEIR): 3

Cruelty towards Life: 3

Cruelty towards God(s), Akua (M7): 3

Psychic Feedback (M7, Telepsi): 3

Occult Wars: 3

Social Assaults, Insults: 2, 3

DESTRUCTION:

Assault with Blades, Knives, Swords: 2, 3
Assault with Gunpowder-based guns: 3
Assault with Arrows, Thrown Weapons: 2
Assault with Explosives, Arson, Laser: 2, 3
Assault with other dangerous items: 2, 3
Hunting Accident: 1, 2
Vehicle Accident: 1, 2
General Destruction: 2, 3
Website Vandalism; Flag Desecration: 2
Graphics Distortion; In-Public urination: 2
Computer Viruses; Computer crimes: 3
Trojans, Hacking programs: 3
Cyber wars: 3
Cyber Terrorism (i.e. Terrorism): 3
Hijacking Vehicles, Airplanes: 3
Car-jacking, stealing vehicle: 3
Disturbing the Peace: 1, 2
Inciting Violence, Profanity: 1, 2, 3
Causing Violence, Hate, Abuse: 2, 3
Bullying, Child Abuse: 2, 3
Retaliation, Blackmail, Threats: 3
Revenge Destruction: 3
Other Destruction: 2, 3

TRAFFIC VIOLATIONS:

Blocking traffic (double-parking): 2

General Traffic Violations: 2, 3

Speeding, recklessness: 2

Following, Cutting in a lane: 2

Not Obeying Traffic Laws: 2, 3

Road Rage: 2, 3

DUI (Drunk Driving): 2, 3

Texting or using Internet while driving: 3

Other Distractions: 2

Ramming, slamming car: 2

Use of car horn to make extra noise: 2

Noisy Car alarms: 2

Evading Cars, or Police: 2, 3

Swerving in traffic: 2

Causing Accidents: 3

Not signaling while turning abruptly: 2

Not paying Fines, Citations: 2, 3

Creating Gestures while driving: 2

Distracting other drivers: 2, 3

Seeking to violate the Law (for fun): 3

Not Yielding to traffic, pedestrians: 3

Not respecting Right of Way: 3

Other Traffic Violations: 2, 3

SEX CRIMES:

Rape, induced: 3

Rape, non-consent: 3

Rape, pillage (town): 3

Rape, Gang: 3

Rape, with Permission: 2

Harassment; Adultery: 2

Sexual Assault; Female Circumcision: 2, 3

Sex Drugs (Chloroform): 2, 3

Date Rape Drug: 3

Date Rape, Misuse of Drone to spy on: 2

With Minor (age. 0-12): 3

With Disabled: 2, 3

With Elderly: 2, 3

With Animals (i.e. Horse): 2, 3

Harassment, multiple: 3

Unwanted Advances: 2, 3

Incest (non-UEIR): 3

Cloning (non-UEIR) 2, 3

Polygamy (non-Pharaoh): 2, 3

Promoting Gender bias: 2

Promoting Bisexuality, etc.: 2

Corrupting the Youth: 2

DEFIANCE:

Overuse of Force (Police): 2, 3
Lying to the UEIR about losing false wars: 3
Failure to adhere to UEIR Laws: 3
Seeking to violate this Law Code: 3
Seeking to Attack the UEIR: 3
Disobeying a command: 3
Perjury in UEIR Courts: 3
Disruption of Society, Insurrection: 3
Causing Corruption, Treason: 3
Causing Dissent among the people: 3
Trying to Overthrow UEIR: 3, 4
Trying to injure or kill UEIR Officers: 3, 4
Anti-UEIR Advertising: 3
Anti-UEIR Anything: 3
Spreading Lies about the UEIR: 2, 3
Spreading Lies about UEIR Officers (S7): 3
Deception of Taxes: 3
Deception in Tax collecting: 2, 3
Overall Defiance: 3
Causing Mischief: 2, 3
Causing Mayhem or Chaos: 3
Causing anti-UEIR propaganda: 3
Supporting Rogue Governments: 3

RELATIONSHIPS

Political Marriage (false union): 2

Marriage for Profit: 2, 3

Profit upon quick Divorce: 2, 3

Elder Marriages (deceptive intent): 2, 3

Ignoring Pre-Nuptial or Dowry: 2

Human + Animal Marriage: 2

Unofficial Marriage: 2, 3

Secular or State Marriage: 2

Hostile Divorce, Marriage: 2, 3

Hostile Take-over (Business): 3

Intimidation, threats (Civil): 2, 3

Hate Crimes: 3

Hate Crimes (Religious): 3

Hate Crimes (Ethnic): 3

Hate Crimes (Disabled): 3

Media / IRS / Police Harassment: 2, 3

Stalking (& Celebrity Stalking): 2, 3

Undesired Union: 2, 3

Aggravation; Domestic Violence: 2, 3

Causing Fear, Paranoia: 2, 3

Causing Depression, Anxiety: 2, 3

Other Relations: 2, 3

Public Disturbance: 1, 2

LAWSUITS:

Unwarranted Lawsuits: 2, 3
Conspiracy Lawsuits: 3
Real Estate, Monetary Lawsuits: 3
Illegal Investigations, selling secrets: 2, 3
Invasion of Privacy: 2, 3
Obtaining Government Data (**On M7**): 3
Frivolous Lawsuits, Data Leaks: 2, 3
Fame Lawsuits: 3
Waiving Right to Sue: 2, 3
Plebes Suing Citizens: 2, 3
Plebes Suing State: 2, 3
Immoral Class Actions: 2, 3
Waiving Moral Rights, TOS: 3
Property Lawsuits (owner): 2, 3
Trespassing, etc.: 2, 3
Simple Assault (Pushing) Suit: 2
Suits against Vizier or Pharaoh: 3
Suits against Consuls (M7): 3
Suits against Council of Elders: 3
Other Suits: 2, 3
False Indictments: 2, 3
Public Scandals (Media): 3

INTELLECTUAL PROPERTY:

Copyright Infringement (paid): 2, 3

Plagiarism (for profit): 2, 3

Obtaining Insignia: 2, 3

Obtaining Insignia (State): 3

Impersonation of Official (**non-Comedy**): 3

Copyright issue (non-Fair Use): 2

Embezzlement (of Book, Music): 3

After the Fact (prior to Law): 2

Non-Body of Evidence: 2

Stolen Patent: 2, 3

Stolen Product (*Eye of the Pharaoh*) : 2, 3

Website Vandalism, Excessive SPAM: 2, 3

Massive Use of Work (paid): 3

Massive Use of Work (unpaid): 2, 3

Poor Compensation (Civil): 2, 3

Not paying author of work: 3

Immoral Publication: 3

Other Infringement: 2, 3

Confidentiality Data Leakage: 3

Selling Trade Secrets: 3

One-Star or Low Product Rating: 2

Trademark Infringement: 2, 3 [®M7]

PROPERTY LAWS:

Trespassing, Vandalism: 2, 3

Deliberate Injury on site: 2, 3

Accidental Injury on property: 1

Neglecting ownership (of Pharaoh): 2

Neglecting Land Lord Rights: 2

Neglecting Tenant's Rights: 2

Not yielding to Pedestrians, Other Life: 2

Not yielding to non-motor Vehicles: 2

Not Yielding to Children (in road): 1, 2

Flooding the Road with People: 2, 3

Riots on Public Land: 2, 3

Violent Protesters (Public): 2, 3

Immoral Confiscation: 2, 3

Causing Fires, Water Damage: 2, 3

Immoral Tax or Levy: 2, 3

Immoral Tax Audits, Fees (IRS): 2, 3

Failure to pay for Walls (repair): 2

Selling Stolen Property (Artifacts): 3

Seizing Stolen Property (non-UEIR): 3

Taxing Public Lands (beach): 1, 2

Wandering while intoxicated: 1, 2

Other violations: 2, 3

AGRICULTURE:

Smuggling items in (snakes, etc.): 2, 3

Ruining Ecosystem: 2, 3

Smuggling via vehicle: 2, 3

Introducing Dangerous Crops: 2

Introducing Dangerous Life, insects: 2

Using Human Manure: (not recycled): 2

Unkempt Sanitation: 2

Causing Floods, Drought (non-Akua): 2

Importing Marijuana, (drugs): 2

Using Marijuana (non-medical), (Smoke): 2

Causing Pollution, smog: 2, 3

Causing Climate Change, smog: 3

Heaping Trash, Garbage: 2

Using Chemical Waste: 2

Not converting waste (recycle): 2

Not recycling usable materials: 2

Littering, Illegal Dumping (cigarettes): 2

Unlicensed Genetic Modification: 2

Not Protecting Rare Life Forms: 2

Polluting Beaches, waterways: 2

Ignoring Customs, Inspection: 2

Other: 2, 3

RELIGIOUS LAWS:

Heresy, Blasphemy (against Divines): 2
Blotting out sacred images, Tikis: 3
Covering Statue Faces with Wax: 2, 3
Destroying Tikis or Idols: 2, 3
Pollution in or near Temples: 2
Attacks on Priesthood, Akua: 3
Imposing "Sharia Laws" on Niihau: 2, 3
Religious Terrorism, Destruction: 3
Stealing (Daily) Temple Offerings: 2
Insulting Priests, Akua, Pharaoh: 2
Desecrating Churches, Temples: 2
Burying Sinners on Holy Ground: 2
Burning "Marijuana Incense": 2
Veiled Threats (to Akua): 2, 3
Destroying Reading Materials: 2
Destroying Ritual Books: 2
Religious Hate Crimes: 3
Inappropriate Use of Royal Seal: 2
Praying against the Akua: 2, 3
Willing people to death (Non-M7): 3
Touching Body of Akua: 3, 4
Not being clean when entering Temple: 2
Other: 2, 3

KAPU (OTHER LAWS):

"Satanic Rituals" of Animal Sacrifices: 2, 3
"Voo-Doo" *or Witchcraft* Astral Assault: 3
Unethical Business Practices: 2
Unethical Financial Services: 2
Denying anyone a Funeral Service: 2
Not cleaning up after a pet (Public): 1, 2
Sabotage, Website-Hostage: 3
Denying Fishing Rights to Natives: 2
Denying Natives their Rights: 2
Self-Employment Taxes: 2
Denying Citizen Lawsuit Rights: 2, 3
Denying Civil Rights: 2
Not Respecting International Law: 1, 2
Not Respecting UEIR Laws: 2
Seceding from State: 1, 2, 3
Disallowing Pharaoh to Edit Laws: 2
Disallowing Vizier to Edit Laws: 2
Disallowing Alii to Edit Laws: 2
Failure to Crown Pharaoh, Alii: 1, 2
Failure to Protect Pharaoh or Alii: 2
Allowing USA (etc.) to elect Pharaoh: 2
Allowing USA (etc.) to interfere in politics: 2
Other: 2, 3

Citizen Civil Rights:

Citizens are registered in Duat or by a Duatian Officer (M7, S7), **not** on *Project Telepsi*. Each Citizen is protected by their Akhu, and can own property, marry or be single, worship their Gods if applicable, join peaceful groups, elect candidates for offices in the Republic, vote, obtain a home in Duat for their Afterlife, uphold the Principals of Ma'at in Society, spend money freely, obey UEIR Laws, etc.

Citizens are protected via *Diplomatic Immunity* in foreign lands, as the **UEIR has Sovereign Immunity** as well to prevent legal actions of foreign States or Nations. Each Citizen has a ***Secret Name*** (in Duat) given to them alone; this may be a name from their previous life via the UEIR in Duat. This is **similar to** a *Social Security number* in USA. **Only Citizens have Secret Names**, and this cannot be forged for the soul resonates with the word.

Plebes are non-Citizens and have limited rights. **Illegal immigrants** after staying one Calendar month in the Province should be registered or refrain from entering UEIR Property or buildings, unless they incur a Fee of $100 USD per day, **or until vacated**. Plebes related to Citizens are called **Knighted Citizens**, and have similar rights as Full Citizens. They just **cannot vote** for UEIR Candidates in the Republic.

Maat Freedoms:

1. **Freedom of Worship.** Citizens are allowed to worship any Egyptian Divine or its compatible equivalent; but not any religion that spawns undesirable behavior, riots, violence or protests, destruction, or fear.
2. **Presses and the Media** must report only Facts and recent information as made known to them by reporters. **Other Media must declare its contents if Fictional** on front and back covers (of any printed material), to prevent misinformation or delusions of its readers.
3. **Freedom of correct speech.** If spoken or recorded as Incorrect speech, it is the fault of the Citizen not the Government.
4. **Equal Rights of all Full Citizens.** Non-Citizens or visitors do not apply here. All Full Citizens have equal rights as specified.
5. **Fair Taxation and Non-Oppressive Taxes or non-confusing tax codes.**
6. **Economy: 2-Currency System.** A Popular Currency (maintained by Citizens) and a National Currency (for Government and Taxes).

7. **Citizenship Awards:** include tax exemption for 1 year.

<u>Other Laws:</u>

8. **Employment: Quality over Quantity.** Quality work will determine advancement not amount of products created.
9. **Teach Self-Control, Self-Restraint** of Citizens.
10. **Learn by Experience**.
11. **Don't gossip** about people in public if said people are suffering from any **paranoia disorders**, as this increases that effect.
12. **Legislation must be written with Wisdom** not on a whim (personal vendetta against society).
13. **Non-violent Crimes** will have the person experience a Deprogramming Session (using drugs & images or computer animation related to the crime) in a Mental Facility, until adapted. Then released after 1 week.
14. **Violent Crimes** will have a month of Deprogramming and be branded with an invisible Bar Code Tattoo or microchip. They will have limited Civil Rights and be given "medication for a fake illness" then released after 2 weeks of observation. They may also be used in forced labor.

<h1 style="text-align:center"><u>Economy:</u></h1>

National Currency:

The *National Currency* of Niihau is the **Kahelelani,** or "Island Shell" (*Pu-pu*), and is valued (paper currency) at the **set value** of a 3-inch strand of that shell. Paper money may be printed as custom business cards, post cards, or as credit cards with **microchips** embedded in them.

Popular Currency:

The *Popular Currency* is valued in **Time Credits**, and will have a **hidden bar code** in invisible ink for tracking purposes (in case of theft, destruction, or misplacement). The paper version (etc.) will be a physical representation of the account of its bearer. Each Citizen will have a Bank Account of Time Credits, or "**Time Bank.**" The account records transactions of goods or services, and each currency will have a starting value of 1.5 Hours of Time / Labor per Bearer; so you can trade Time Credits via the Time Bank and print out the paper version for physical transactions and the bar code will record this. PCs are each valued in *100 units of National Currency (One Caesar = 100 Barternotes).

Pharaoh's Duties:

Pharaoh is to promote and **uphold the concept of Ma'at** on Earth, and to oversee Legal Matters, Social Matters & Gatherings (religious or secular), attend ceremonies of State (awards, speeches, foreign events), oversee the enforcement of Law & Order, and spend taxes or buy items.

The **General Rule** is: whatever Pharaoh likes is permitted or Legal, and whatever Pharaoh dislikes is non-permitted or Illegal. Pharaoh as an instrument of Ma'at has **Sovereign Immunity**. Pharaoh is Chief Land owner (owns virtually everything) and can distribute taxes or other revenue to the State and to the People directly.

Every 30th year of Pharaoh's Reign is the event called a **Heb-Sed Festival (or Jubilee)**, whereby Pharaoh is tested, physically and or mentally, to determine fitness to continue ruling. If not, then another Pharaoh will be elected in his or her place. This may also occur every 15th year if necessary. The test can be anything from simple to moderate in complexity; a short run around a track, or a mental quiz or puzzle that the common Citizen can perform.

The **Council of Elders** is comprised of the eldest able adult (male or female) of each nuclear family. The Council decides on civil or criminal matters and can elect the Alii or Pharaoh via Secret Ballot. Vizier and other

offices may be appointed by Pharaoh. The
Council should consist of Residents from or on
Niihau, and chosen representatives of Pharaoh
or his associates, family, friends, or other
Native Hawaiians or Portuguese members.

Native Rights are: allowing Natives from
Niihau acreage or space for a home or
residence, Free Fishing Rights, space for a
Garden or Farm to grow food or fruit trees,
right to be buried on Future Necropolis or be
relocated there, right to wear traditional
clothing, right to practice Native Culture
without reprisal from State of Hawaii or
Christian Missionaries, right to make cultural
products (Niihau shell leis, flower leis,
weapons or tools, etc.), right to an education
in a school, college, or distance-learning class
room; right to clean and purified water, and
the right to own and care for pets.

The Alii will maintain these rights or
add to them as needed. Future Pharaohs (or
M7) may add or edit this Document to conform
to the **Status Quo**. Espionage by non-citizens
on citizens is highly illegal, and is considered
stalking, harassment, invasion of privacy, etc.

The Pharaoh's Court includes his
Family, servants, officers or overseers, friends,
advisors, Senators, Princes or heirs, secretary,
High Priests, Viceroy of Military, Vizier or
Prime Minister, Banker, Accountant, Security,
Lawyers, Imperial Guard, Temples, and place
of residence.

<h1 style="text-align:center">Holidays:</h1>

January 1 (New Year's Day); **March 14** (Caesar Day); **May 9** (Howard Carter / M7 Day); **June 21** (Summer Solstice); **July 5** (*Akua Niihau Founding Day*); **August 31** (Caligula Day); **November 4** (Tut Day); **November 26** (Ancestor Day); **December 25** (Wadjet Traveling Day, & Christmas).

National Anthem: *Good Vibrations* (Beach Boys song); Conch Shell (1.5 Minutes).

National Stone: Emerald or lava rock.

National Bank: *Bank of Niihau* (Time Bank):

State Deities: Kane, Ku, Asaris (Osiris), Ptah, AmonRa, Lono, Hathor, Isis, Maat, & Akua M7.

National Motto: *"When Science fails, Fantasy prevails."*

Oath of Office: *"Hail AmonRa, King of the Gods; may he be victorious always."*

Official Color: *White, with hint of Green.*

National Drink: *Half & Half* (Part Lemonade, Part Iced [Green or Mint] Tea); Arnold Palmer.

National Fruit: Passion Fruit or Guava.

Official Transportation: Kayak Boat.

Energy: Solar, Wind, Wave Motion Generation.

Chief Export: Recyclables, Farmed goods.

Chief National Products: Books (M7), Crafts (Shell Leis), Archaeology Research (on sites), charcoal, honey, textiles, tourism, etc.

Main Income: (Non-UEIR) US Military Missile Base facility (rented); paid admission for tourism or hunting, Archaeology Museums (future), UEIR Taxes.

Entertainment: (Mainland) Computer games; (Island) Hunting, Fishing, Water sports, Luau Feasts, Fire Dance, Hula Dance, Hawaiian Culture, Niihau Arts & Crafts, Lei Making, etc.

Capital City: M7 City (Island) on Niihau (as of 2017 CE).

Population: (Mainland) unspecified; (Island) about 134 residents.

Size: 18 x 6 square miles approx. with other land estates annexed (M7), (**Ni'ihau only**); included: Niihau (2000), Lanai (2015), Kahoolawe (2016), etc. 18 x 13 sq. miles (**Lana'i**), 11 x 6 sq. miles (**Kahoolawe**).

Ni'ihau = (Nee-hee-how), **Lana'i** (Lay-Na-ee), **Kaho'olawe** = (Kah-Oh-Oh-lah-wee).

Chapter 5: Pharaoh's Duties:

Royal Scepters, Regalia, or Dress:

Each Pharaoh may wear traditional Ancient (Pharaonic) Egyptian costume or attire while in duration of said office. This may be modified to Hawaiian or modern standards.

The **Nemes** head cloth is usually striped horizontally on a rectangle of cloth, usually cotton or synthetic. It is folded so that two ends drop over each shoulder, giving it a sloped appearance.

The **Leopard print Sash** is also appealing to Pharaohs or High Priests and Lector Priests, symbolic of Egyptian or Mayan Priests who controlled Nature with their willpower.

The **Crooked Scepter and the Flail** may be worn as a garment pin, or held as scepters, one in each hand, crisscrossing the chest like an "X." This is worn on State Ceremonies or funerals, in reference of Lord Osiris, the God and Judge of the Dead. The "X" is a universal symbol of the dead (Osiris; Akua Spirits).

A crown, diadem, or Ring may be worn usually on the right third finger, symbolizing royalty. The crown or Ring may be of gold or other metals or colorful stones. Pharaohs also wear colorful robes or capes, or in modern, double-breasted business suits.

Citizens Status:

There are 5 Classes of People in the Pharaocracy of Niihau:

1. **Akua Class – the Sovereign & his Family, and other divine people.**
2. **Nobles Class [Ali'i] – Friends of the Sovereign & <u>Residents</u> of the Islands (Native Hawaiians, & Niihau).**
3. **Citizens [Kupa] – Non-resident, a general class of people. Includes Natives of Niihau, Kauai & Lanai.**
4. **Plebeian – Non-Citizens, or Visitors to the Pharaocracy.**
5. **Shabtis – Reduced Status due to Crime or Debts.**

Akua Class:

Akua are traditionally divine people (i.e. Psychic, super-psychic, **deity**) who were alive among the Native Hawaiians and interacted with them. As Pharaoh is traditionally considered Divine, s/he is an Akua; the Egyptian word for Akua may be Akhu, or "Angel." **Akua are tax-exempt.** This includes the **Akua M7's Family & close Friends**.

Nobles Class:

Nobility here are the *Friends of Pharaoh*, including any close allies; it also includes the Native people who "came with the Island of Niihau." [**Resident Niihau'ans**] Nobles (Ali'i) are exempt from Income Taxes.

Citizen Class:

A Citizen of the Pharaocracy of Niihau is a Native of Niihau, Lanai, Kauai or Molokai living elsewhere, naturalized by M7, or a patron of M7's books. In USA one has to read the History & Government of America for Naturalized Citizenship. Citizens have reduced Taxes (income tax is 10% per month), but at the moment this is **optional should the USA pay its debts to me** so I won't need to charge taxes; **otherwise** the taxes remain in effect. The USA owes M7 somewhere in the hundreds of billions of US$, according to CIA / a source (*from UEIR Taxes*).

Plebeian Class:

Plebes are non-citizens, or Visitors to Niihau. Plebes if in the Country longer than 1 month will pay Income Taxes of 10% to 15% per month thereafter starting on the first day after the first month of visit. US Military for the Missile Base are **exempt**, as this base is leased to Niihau.

Shabtis Class:

In Lieu of a Prison or other punishments, this is a reduced status of person for Crime or Debts. If a person is bankrupt for more than 6 months, or owes debts to the Pharaocracy of Niihau, or violates Major Crime laws, said person will become a Shabty Class status until this is removed upon redemption. Shabtis are also foreigners who try to steal parts of Niihau or anyone trying to overthrow it, violate our laws or customs, investigate it with malicious intent, etc. Shabtis may not vote, hold public or official office, collect State welfare or social benefits (to prevent the State from paying their debts), or enlist in the Military. Shabtis may appeal this status after about 1 year if the Courts agree on some form of compensation [**Paid Fines**] in their situation.

<u>Notes:</u>

Nobles have the potential to become Sovereign (Pharaoh) should no heir is found or appointed successor by the previous Pharaoh. If No Nobles are available, this responsibility is sent to Citizens who may elect a Sovereign via a **random Lottery of qualified individuals**. **Qualifications for Pharaoh** may include: a University Degree (B.A., B.S., M.A., M.S., Ph.D., etc.), high moral values, stamina or physical qualities, knowledge of Ancient Civilizations & of Niihau History, and leadership skills. Any runoff election where 2 or more candidates are available, the outcome may be decided by a competition of winning 2 out of 3 **Senet** Board Games. **Senet** is an Ancient Egyptian board game similar to Backgammon using *Chance* as a decisive factor. Reading **this Book may be** considered for Citizen status, though I prefer it be one of my novels.

Citizens and above classes may choose a **Patron Deity** as a **prefix** to their personal name. Patron Deity names may be either Native Hawaiian or Ancient Egyptian in origin (gods, goddesses, deified people). **Examples**: (Male): Horus, Osiris, Anubis, Thoth, Ptah, Bes, Nu, Seth, Amun, Ra, Amun-Ra, Nefertum, Sobek; Ku, Kane, etc. (Female): Isis, Mut, Nephthys, Maat, Hathor, Tauret, Shai, Sakhmet, Selqet; Pele, etc.   So this is read like: Horus Michael, Isis Mary, Anubis Harry, Thoth John, Ku Matthew, etc. **Citizens and Nobles** may use a **Cartouche** for their names, but **only Akua** class may use a rectangular **Serekh** for their names.

Notes:

Niihau = July 5, 2000 **($2B)**;
Lanai = October 29, 2015 **($12 B)**; L.E. (CEO).
Kahoolawe = December 6, 2016 **($26M)**.
(UEIR) = February 6, 2016 **($90B)**.
Molokai = August 7, 2017 **($16B)**.
All were acquired legally via UEIR Taxes.

Citizen's responsibilities include a **Pledge of Loyalty** (similar to Pledge of Allegiance in USA), said at four different times of day. This may be said to a flag (sign of deity) or stone/wooden Tiki statue, or in a circle of stones.

1. At Morning: "Hail Kheper-Ra! With Peace and Friendship."
2. At Noon: "Hail Ra! With a good life and success."
3. At Evening: "Hail Atum-Ra (or Tmu-Ra)! With prosperity and good luck."
4. At Night: "Hail Osiris-Ra! With compassion and forgiveness."

The Eldest and most Able Child or Adult of each House or Family may join the **Council of Elders** as an Initiate. The Council of Elders [Jury] oversees the Courts of Law, Ancestor's rights, and acts like an Advisory to Pharaoh (i.e. Senate). Citizens may adhere to a Moral Code of Law, while **Plebes** may adhere to the **Provincial Laws of the UEIR (Code Caesar 4.0**). The Laws of PON may be enforced by Security Forces, Pharaoh's Magic, or via Kauai Island when available.

<u>Important:</u>

Pharaohs may be appointed by the Senate from a list of qualified Citizens, by the Elder Council, by another Pharaoh, or via random drawing in a Lottery. Pharaohs may be either gender.

Government:

The Top Position is of course the **Pharaoh**. Below this are the **Vizier(s), & High Priest**, then following are the **Royal Overseers, Nomarchs** (Governors), **Scribes, Artists & Craftspeople**, and then the Food producers or **Farmers**. The Vizier is a Prime Minister. Depending on the size of this Government, one Vizier is necessary, with a deputy PM if needed. The High Priest handles all elements relating to making the gods happy (weather deities or "Elemental Chronokinetics"), and collecting donations & prayers from the people. The Royal Overseers are like a Board of Directors. Nomarchs are governors; I may only require one for Niihau, to run day-to-day activities. Scribes or Writers, Secretaries, or general bureaucracy, assist with creating legal forms, printing, newspapers / newsletters, reporting news, etc. Artists & Craftspeople are assigned to creating Niihau jewelry (leis), murals, wooden crafts, etc. The Food production crew or Farmers (possibly in Kauai real estate – M7) will tend to the storage of food and other products; if wheat is allowed there [Kauai or Niihau], we can store it in granaries for use as currency (in exports).

Royal Overseers:

Overseer of Treasury: Basically it is an **accountant**, in charge of finances for the government, oversees currency and taxes.

Overseer of Military: Viceroy. Chief of Security, oversees immigration and tourists, military, police/security, robots, Public Relations, port security, helicopter port, energy, media, terrorism, aircraft security, and foreign governments.

Overseer of Bureaucracy: Chief Scribe. Secretary of State, oversees legislation, office work of King, reports to King, national security issues, takes notes at meetings, updates websites, email, & other items. **Keeper of the Royal Seal / Insignia.**

Overseer of Agriculture. Chief of farming and ranches. Oversees granaries in city-state, water, sanitation, irrigation, recycling, environmental issues, wildlife habitats, eco-farming, genetic modified food, vineyards, orchards, greenhouses, foreign imports, etc.

Overseer of the Media/Technocrat. Overseer of entertainment, television, film, Museums, Archaeologists, sports, printing press (books, magazine, newspaper, currency), concerts, festivals, videos, research technology, **Communications Officer**, etc.

Overseer of Theocracy: Kahuna Priest. Chief of Temples/Churches, Native issues, Akua, education, marriage, ceremonies, customs, intelligence gathering, covert assignments, ambassadors, & civil services.

Overseer of the Courts: Chief Justice. From the Elder Council is a representative or Senior Elder who is caretaker of the Legal System when Pharaoh is unavailable. While a General Forum may decide Court cases, the Elder Council presides over major crimes, lawsuits, legal threats from foreign nations (USA, Japan), environmental issues, pollution, family issues, Natives of Niihau, and other information. Each Chief Justice *should have* a University degree in some form of Law (USA law degrees are permitted when dealing with American tourists) or Criminal Justice; that is "*should have*" but is not required.

Overseer of Foreign Relations/ Foreign Affairs & Immigration: Emir or Sultan: Each Emir or Sultan is, as you may guess, representative of Foreign Affairs. The foreign affairs correspondent may dress in exotic clothing to give a good impression to foreign Heads of State that wish diplomatic ties to Niihau, and may have a private stipend to pay for traveling. This office may oversee tourism and Entrance Visas separate from the Viceroy.

King's duties: writes legislation when necessary, gives orders, edicts. Can deport anyone back to Kauai / Mainland, supreme Judge of the Court(s), oversees some entertainment, oversees economy, sets prices & taxes, can declare peace/war/ sanctions on foreigners, can arrest enemy or foreign nationals. Pharaoh is Chief Priest of all the Akua, Chief Temple Master, overseer of Temple economy. Can spend taxes and funding. Can oversee research or space technology. Can create (robot) military or police officers. Can collect tribute. Can oversee media and attend foreign parties or meetings. Etc.

As an **Absolute Monarch**, Pharaoh is **not** limited in power with regard to Laws & Order. His word is Law; anything Pharaoh likes is legal, anything he dislikes is illegal, without need for a written law code unless Pharaoh wishes to delegate this power to the Viceroy temporarily.

Agricultural Inspection to or from the Islands would charge on exports the same as Sales Tax (5% of value of item in US$D). If someone swims from another island to bypass this rule, they are charged 10% of item, though it is unlikely this will occur. Taxes may be paid in Pupu Currency, US$D, Barter, Kahelelani,

Gold/Emeralds/Platinum/Silver, Pupu shells, or via Island Produce. **Hunting Tax** is $10 per hunter, $50 per kill (of wild boar/goat, etc.).

Niihau Industries:

Formerly a Cattle & Goat Ranch (said to have closed in 1999), the island also had (before 2002) provided charcoal from trees, commercial fishing, honey cultivation, and cultural Shell Lei making.

Proposed industries by M7:

Niihau can become farmland, using the leftover byproducts of ranching for fertilizer and irrigation. Mostly a desert-like island, the central region is about Sea-Level with a mountain along one side. Stone walls made of Lava rock should protect against tidal waves coming from Japan or Hawaii, built along the coast and in future Cities. Lava rock Docks or Piers are also ideas, protecting a harbor for ships. Farmland would include **foreign plants**: Wheat, Flax, (Cotton), Cocoa, Grapes, Soy beans, Barley, Oats, Corn, (Sugar Cane or Sugar Beets), Lettuce, Yams, Chick peas, Date palms, Carob beans, Papyrus, Frankincense and Lotus flowers. Some of these exist on Kauai in hotel resorts. Wheat, Corn, Oats, Barley are for **cereals, bread, and beer making**. Cocoa, Carob and Sugar Cane are **for candy making**. Grapes and Dates are for **wine making (Date Beer** with Barley). Papyrus is for **paper and**

boat making (etc.). Lotus flowers & Frankincense are **for perfume making or incense**. Flax and Cotton are for **clothing and textiles / paper**. These crops may exist **in Greenhouses** rather than in open fields to prevent contamination of "Native plants." I chose these from Ancient Egyptian industries because Niihau is mostly desert, and thus hospitable in climate.

Recycling is an industry of modern times. Materials can be used again via recycling (melting metals or glass and reshaping them into ingots, paper and cardboard recycled in similar manner and plastics too). Niihau can import recyclables directly from Kauai or initially to start production. Recycled paper can be used for newspapers, currency / money, restaurant menus, packaging, toilet paper, computer paper, etc. Recycled glass can be utilized for windows, bottles, computer screens, art work, etc. Recycled metal can be shaped for coins, technology, containers, packaging, bowls, silver ware, etc. Recycled plastics are useful as identity or credit cards, plates, technology, etc. The less trash exists, the better is the environment.

Museum Curators & Archaeology is useful, because Niihau has an unwritten history that needs recording. Excavations should exist prior to building. The history of the Natives should be recorded, including their native crafts (flower, shell & feather leis, whicker wood, or weaving).

Commercial Fishing is limited to 4 large fish per person per day to prevent overkill of the fish population. Fish hatcheries are limited by population, **or** 10 fish per person per day, whichever is less. **Endangered Species** are not to be harvested of course, and any tampering with them is illegal, and would revoke a fishing license for 1 year if reported.

Budget:

The **Annual Budget** is dependent on available funds or income to the State.   This may come from owned corporations, businesses, taxes, fines, import or export revenue, Bureaucracy forms, other dues, Temple donations, offerings, crafts sales, Missile Base Lease, Hotels (**on Kauai**), entrance visas, Bank profits, stocks or bonds, etc. Also included is what the US Government **owes to M7's Estate** after 1993 CE. Employees and offices are paid in equal portions to prevent envy. This amount is drawn from a general pool of resources / or revenue / income.

<u>**Employees**</u>: (Per $100M **estimate** amount **per year** or allocation, in US$ Dollars):

Royal Overseers: $1 M each (or $15M total estimate).

Nomarch: $5M each (1).

High Priest: $10M.

Vizier: $15M each (1).

Elder Council: $10M total.

Scribes/Bureaucracy: $10M total.

Artists/Craftspeople: $10M total.

Farmers: $5M total.

Pharaoh: $20M.

<u>**Offices:**</u> (Per $400M **estimate** amount per year or allocation, in US$ Dollars):

[Sum total spent per year estimate is $500M]

CORE FUNDS:

Bank of Niihau: $50M (savings is $30M, loans are $10M, employees are remainder).

Recycling: $10M.

Sanitation & Water filtration/Desalination: $20M.

Solar power & Wind (Energy): $10M.

Agriculture/Ranch/Food: $30M.

Health & Medicine: $20M.

Education: $15M.

Infrastructure (roads, trees, décor, plumbing, airport): $15M.

Security: $40M.

Fire Prevention, Life Guards, & other Civil Services: $30M total.

Disaster Relief Fund (Insurance; hurricanes, etc.): $50M total.

Emergency utilities, electric generators, etc.: $25M total.

Transportation (Boats, helicopters, solar cars, monorails): $10M.

Sum total: $325M.

ADD-ONS:

State Museums, Libraries, Edifices, Monuments (Maintenance): $5M.

Temples (Akua, Kahuna Priests) Fund: $10M.

Arts & Sciences Fund: $5M.

Technology & Medical Research: $5M.

Insignia Design, Currency, Other Servants: $5M.

Special Projects Fund: $5M.

(Natives) Welfare: $35M.

Treasury (Saved): $5M.

LEFTOVERS are added to a general pool if unspent and each category will then draw funds from it when necessary, or such funds will be available for the following year in each category.

Core Funds are the required Revenue, while Add-Ons are not essential in case of recessions or lack of funds. Government can also be a volunteer-run administration in case funding is not available. Amounts may increase in case of a surplus budget, or decrease if $500M is not available using a lesser number (like $50M or $500k).

(USA Pres. Trump used this idea in his 2017 Budget).

Housing on Niihau:

Once a **City-State** is constructed in the midst of the Island or wherever location is safest, housing may be built with internal plumbing & sanitation. The City-State would be modeled after a standard Egyptian arrangement (see Pharaonic Egypt), with a retaining security wall surrounding it made of stone-bricks (stone-faced bricks or interlocking bricks as found in Mayan Civilization in Mexico / Central-America). *The following description may be somewhat extreme.*

My plans included building a **city-state in central Niihau**. This city-state would be several square miles in diameter, with perimeter walls and reservoirs. It would have 3 Temples (one Ancient Egyptian, one Native Hawaiian, and one Church). The city-state would be **divided into 7 parts**: a central core for government buildings, surrounded by the other 6 parts. One part would be for light industry, 2 parts for farming, 2 parts for residences, and 1 part for a city park (near Temples) with artificial waterfalls/lakes. The **government buildings** would include: robot security, the Palace, marketplace, medical clinic, high school, Junior College (distant learning from Oahu), newspaper/Internet Café, stores, Museums, library, Roman Bath house/swimming pools, Energy Center (solar, wind, etc.); water filter site, **recycling center**, the 3 Temples, solar monorail port, helicopter port, Bank, Printing Press (currency, books, media); Granaries, warehouses, and some office buildings. Farming would have greenhouses and irrigation (foreign crops to island). **Farms** should have some form of grain (wheat, rice, corn, etc.), fruits, vegetables, coffee / cocoa, sugarcane (for alternative fuel to export), nuts, flax/cotton (for fabric/currency), incense trees (for temples), and native trees. The **City Park** would have flowers, artificial waterfalls / lakes / pools, monuments (obelisks, small pyramids or statues), benches, pathways, and grasses. The **residences** would **include medium houses or apartments**, with some land surrounded by privacy walls or screens. The **robot security** would include automatons that speak in Native Hawaiian, English, Japanese, & other languages, and have keyboards to type in languages / voice recognition, GPS, camera, and have electric shock (minor) to deter criminals from entering the City or Isle. The **Palace** would be the Sovereign's residence (M7). It would include several levels (3 above ground), and also serve as a visitor's lodging (similar to a hotel with restaurant, information center, rooms, laundry, swimming pool/hot tubs, and other features). The **light industry** would include: textiles / clothing, food production, arts / crafts (shell leis, sculpture, beads), paper, honey (native), chocolate/coffee, sugar / Ethanol, incense, recycled products (paper, glass, metal, plastic = exports), books, perfume (flowers), and sea salt. The **Museums** would be for locals and tourists (art, artifacts, & local history). <u>**Water would be imported from Kauai, as Niihau is a desert.**</u> Cities or Towns may be 2 to 3 square miles in size on Niihau.

Honorary Titles:

Honorary Titles can be purchased (used for distinction in Hawaii or Micronation **via an annual fee**), as a way to support Niihau's future economy. Call it a "**donation**" to Niihau and in return you may be called whatever title purchased, unless you abuse it of course (in which case you cannot use it until next time).
Pharaoh title is reserved for the Sovereign, as is Queen (for Sovereign's girlfriend or wife). Although it is doubtful Pharaoh will ever have children (at present time), *Prince* can be purchased for 1 year each time.

A limit of 3 titles per person per year is allowed. The word "Honorary" precedes each title.

Sir = as in Knighthood or better than Master (Mr.), is common for adults. = $1000 each.
Lord or Lady = $10,000 each.
Scribe (writer) = $15,000 each.
Divine Scribe = $25,000 each. **Setem Priest** = $50,000 each.

Kahuna (Expert/Priest) = $74,000 each.
Baron (High Level Vassal or Knight) = $100k each.
Vice-Chancellor = $150,000 each.
Vizier (Prime Minister) = $250,000 each.
Imperator = $500,000 each.
Consul = $740,000 each.
Consul Premier = $900,000 each.
Prince / Princess = $1,000,000 each.
Laurel Caesar / His Excellency = $5M each.
Illustrious Caesar / His Royal Excellency = $10M each.
Honorary Akua of Niihau = $25M each.

> **Example**: "Honorary Scribe Michael,"
> Or: "Honorary Lady Mary."

*All prices are in US$D payable in cash/check to Niihau **or** the Author **via Niihau**. If via Niihau, 50% of all sales will go to support the people of Niihau (**after someone informs them of this**).* This is not the same as the Patron Deity for Citizens; Honorary Titles are an **option** for Plebeians or Citizens alike, not Shabtis.

(*Excerpt from "The Pharaocracy of Niihau" is Copyright © MC 2011, © 2009 MC*)

Chapter 6:

Pharaohism (Official Religion)

The **official religion** of the UEIR is called **Pharaohism**. This is the creation of the office of **Pharaoh**, a type of **Divine King**. A Pharaoh is chief high Priest of **all** the Egyptian Gods and Goddesses, Angels (Akhu), and other spiritual beings who influence the World. A Pharaoh is chief legislature and enforcer, using his (or her) Divine Abilities. A Pharaoh is the Judge of the actions of the people, and intermediary between Duat (Afterlife, or Heaven) and Earth (the Living). A Pharaoh is the ceremonial head of the Military; basically the same as a President of the United States of America, *but with more* power. As Power can corrupt the Living, a Pharaoh must adhere to the **concept of Ma'at** and uphold its virtues.

The Gods are basically entities that exude *Chronokinetic Energy*, so they are seen as power sources. By venerating **all** the Gods and Goddesses, a Pharaoh can control **all** of Nature. This divine vocabulary is the names of these entities, and when uttered or written by Pharaoh, the sacred attributes work like Magic. Pharaoh may become telepathic as a result of this practice. Telepathy can be **fun** to influence peoples' actions remotely.

The Gods and Goddesses are worshiped or venerated in **Marble Temples**. They are granted real estate to provide for the daily offerings sent in Temples. The offerings are considered Tax revenue to the Temples. Unused offerings are given to **charity**. 1/5 of Offerings are payment to the Priesthood, the remainder (after the Gods consume it, if available) is stored in Temple Granaries (Bank).

Offerings to Temples may include: packaged food and drink, coins, real estate, gems, fresh flowers, perfumed incense, books & music, artwork, technology, clothing, soap or body wash (unguents), currency or gift cards, etc.

Temples resemble Gardens in their architecture. The pillars supporting the ceiling are in the shape of plants or flowers found in Ancient Egypt, the ceiling is painted blue with (glow-in-the-dark) stars in Constellations. Temples may include libraries, Colleges, Museums, storage rooms, Priest offices, ceremonial rooms, worship centers, Planetariums, Banks, and Court rooms. Temples are also decorated with statues of Pharaohs or sphinxes, gods, or animals; obelisks and pyramids, and colorful murals.

The act of Prayer may be silent telepathy or formal, as with holding one's hand over the heart with the other hand raised and bent slightly at the elbow.

Prayers recited may be in the ancient tongue (*Ancient Egyptian or Coptic*), or in common language. Prayers are also written in paper scrolls. **In Ancient Egypt** there was a **Hell** (Aset Tchabet, or Place of Punishment), a **Satan** (called Sata, chapter 87 of the BOTD), a **Christ** (QRST), **and a Creator God** (Ptah). There were **Angels** (Akhu, or Akua in Ancient Hawaii/Polynesia), though now confused with the other Gods and Goddesses. **St. Michael the Archangel was called Horus the Avenger**. **In Islam**, people worship by surrendering themselves to Allah (God); in Egypt this was done **for Pharaoh** by his conquered vassals, where they are seen 'kissing the floor before Pharaoh.' **Paradise** is the *Fields of Offerings*. **Heaven** is called Pet (PT), represented by the glyph for the Sky. The "evil Pharaohs" from **the Quran** were the **Hyksos** of the 13th to 17th Dynasties. The God(s) of the Jews, Christians and Muslims can be found in Ancient Egypt, if you look closely…

<u>**Examples**</u> of Egyptian Prayer (or what moderns call Magic):

For causing Rain:

DUA TEFNUT DI ANKH HOTEPU

For causing Storms:

DUA TEFNUT SET DI ANKH HOTEPU

For causing Winds:

DUA AMUN DI ANKH HOTEPU

For causing Prosperity:

DUA AMONRA AA

For causing lasting Peace:

DUA ASARIS NEB-ANKH AA DI ANKH HOTEPU

For excellent Health or to cure diseases:

DUA SAKHMET IMHOTEP AA DI ANKH URP

To be protected from danger or evil:

DUA BES AA DI ANKH HOTEPU URP NEFRU

To protect one's home and belongings:

DUA BASTET PER-ANKH DI ANKH HOTEPU

4-22-2017. **For Niihau Island:**

http://us.blastingnews.com/tech/2017/04/uc-berkeley-researchers-find-new-way-to-extract-water-from-the-air-001630665.html

I want someone to build 100 of these **water-conversion devices** once they are fully developed for the desert island of Niihau, as owned by M7. Another solution is to import bottled water from M7's estate(s) in Kauai, the one with the reservoir. Solid waste would form fertilizer for farming on Niihau with used water from plumbing. Build some water **cisterns** to contain the water. Ocean water can be useful in sanitation for toilets, as this is not for drinking purposes. Niihau is mostly a desert. It can be made into a thriving farming community. **Archaeology sites** are another **economic factor** on Niihau, for exporting artifacts to a Museum on Kauai or Niihau, as owned by M7. Plants that can grow on Niihau should be researched, including those for making medicine, food, clothing, or technology resources; the University of Hawaii can help with this. **The USA Navy Base on Niihau** should be updated to intercept anything fired from **North Korea**.

5-1-2017. (WH):

Re: **Kim Jong Un - North Korea**

If you allow the Supreme Leader of North Korea into the United States for Diplomacy, may I recommend you keep him here until all unlawful prisoners of NK be released to the USA? Or at least ransom North Korea until they surrender their nuclear weapons? I have experience with North Korea. In 1994 (The CIA can inform you about this) I wrote on the Internet anti-NK statements. Within 24 hours, I arrived in Maui, Hawaii. The top headlines of the Maui News read, "Headless Beast dies in North Korea, Kim Il-Sung dead of heart attack." I also caused Un to become sick a while ago, and cursed his missile attempts. "Hail Sakhmet and Horur! May the leader of North Korea (Kim Jong Un) suffer misfortune and failure! So says the Supreme Eternal Pharaoh of the United States of America!"

5-15-2017. (WH):

Re: Shelters?

http://www.northwestsheltersystems.com/bomb-shelters/

Can you build some shelters along the Pacific Coast?

Since the (first) Cold War, shelters were dismantled when the **USSR** fell. Now we may need some.

Also build some in Hawaii.

(Fake News) Alternative Factual UEIR Purchases for 2017: (My Blog):

1. We bought a Cruise Line for $6B USD (UEIR Taxes).

2. 10 New Egyptian Temples, built on the Island of Tamery ($150M).

3. Three New Imperial Cities ($10B each).

4. A Nuclear Generator ($100M) for energy.

5. A Solar Energy Company ($2B).

6. Part of Northern Jerusalem, under Pharaoh's Mound located some 1.5 miles underground ($15B).

7. 7 Egyptian Pyramids in Egypt (ranging from $100M to $5B).

8. 40 Miles of Farmland ($300M).

9. 15 Miles of Coastal land ($150M).

10. Part of the old USSR MIR Space Station, salvaged in Space prior to reentry ($10M).

11. 124 small Islands, mostly range from 400 acres to 4 Miles Diameter ($400M).

12. An Asteroid for future Space Mining Colonies ($50M).

13. Land reclaimed in Antarctica (40 Miles); ($50M).

14. A Book Publishing Company for M7 ($1.5B).

(Alternative Facts = Misinformation)

If the Chemical Weapons "attack" in Syria was **Fake News**, it worked by enraging the USA President into attacking the Syrian Army. Now consider that any Fake News can do this, the USA National Security is at risk for causing reactions against innocence.

So... This is some **Fake News** that will garner some attention:

!! BREAKING NEWS !!

North Korean Leader, **Kim Jong Un**, was ASSASSINATED by a Sudden Inexplicable Disease! The Disease ravaged Un's body suddenly, causing convulsions, headaches, high fever, chills, and hallucinations. One of his visions was the image of his Grandfather, Kim Il-Sung, who as you know was also killed by Lord S7 in 1994 via the Internet, and North Korea was plagued by Drought and Famine for

7 years thereafter. North Korea then experienced a 9.0 r/s Earthquake following Un's Sudden Demise.

- M7, 2017.

6-05-2017.

Re: UEIR to buy Mexico with UEIR Taxes

If the UEIR wishes to purchase Mexico:

1. UEIR will legalize and regulate Drugs in Mexico. This will create jobs and strip power from the Drug Cartels in the Drug Wars in Mexico. Drugs will be grown in Mexico and exported as Medicine, not entertainment.

2. Increase mining of precious metals in Mexico and other minerals or Oil.

3. Make people want to go to Mexico instead of leaving for USA (no need for a Wall).

4. Update Legal system in Mexico (UEIR Code Caesar).

5. Reform building codes to comply with Earthquake safety and stability.

6. Increase solar and wind energy collection for all new buildings in Mexico. Sell surplus energy for profit.

7. Reform Government into Corporation type Democracy, with Directors as officers.

8. Make Currency based on Stock Market performance.

9. Reduce unnecessary taxes. Create a 15% Corporation Tax except for Nationalized Businesses. Charge an exit fee for immigrants from Mexico to USA; payable by Families still living in Mexico being supported by immigrants to USA.

10. UEIR is considered Divine Intervention, not a replacement of Government. Mexico will still be Democratic.

11. Create Film Industry, Online Colleges with Distance Learning, Drone Factories, Replicas of Native Monuments or artifacts as a regulated industry, and a Director of Archaeology in the Government.

12. Create an Intelligence and Counter-terrorism Department in Mexico.

13. Register all Citizens with Genetic information on all passports and driver licenses. Use cheek cells to determine DNA for entrance exams. Maintain this database offline and online to prevent being hacked by criminals.

14. Create Artificial Intelligence on Robot Police Officers and other technology.

UEIR Charity - from UEIR Tax Revenue (M7):

($1 Billion USD - Foundation Deposit):

1. To support relief from Natural Disasters and Human Actions.

2. To find solutions and vaccines to popular diseases and social conditions.

3. To research technology in developing Nations.

4. To lift Poverty by supporting job training in poor countries.

5. To distribute surplus food from Farms that would otherwise be destroyed and send it to

Food Banks in USA and in Foreign Countries (as a Peace Offering).

6. To support NASA and the U.S. Postal Service.

7. To support Recycling and Solar Energy programs in poor countries and those affected by social conditions.

© 8-22-2016, M7

7-06-2017 (WH):

Re: Niihau Island (town = 2 to 3 square miles):

All Architecture on Niihau shall be in the style of Ancient Egyptian buildings (for Pharaocracy of Niihau), and must be resistant to Hurricanes and wild boars (steel-reinforced concrete, jigsaw puzzle bricks), this includes Pylon Gateways, walls, trapezoid exteriors with painted floral columns, obelisks, Sphinx statues, Seated Pharaoh Statues, and interior murals. The following buildings for the central Town are necessary: Medical Clinic, Community Center, General Store, Bank (with island currency), Security (includes Firemen and Police), K-12 School with separate buildings, Churches & Egyptian Temples, Warehouses, recycling center, Solar Powered Generators, Water wells and cisterns (with purification filters), Houses for residents, Trade school, Dock access with Ferry boat, Archaeology Museum (for local artifacts), Central Park (with statues), integrated sewer drains, solar monorail, and Fertilizer Sanitation facility. The revenue sent to residents can help with this, or use UEIR Taxes. Thank you.

M7 of the UEIR, 2017.

Added buildings (optional): Restaurants, Postal Office, Library, extend Navy Base with airport and hangers (for helicopters and drones), Farms (outside town), Customs/Immigration office, More Stores, Marketplace, Art Gallery, solar reverse-Osmosis facility, Forum (Court), Castle (Palace to be built on Kauai), Internet Cafe, Solar self-driving cars, wind mills, multi-level greenhouses, Government Offices, Hotel with golf course, **Anti-missile battery to intercept ICBMs (on Navy Base),** football/baseball field & salt-water swimming pools (for school), radio station.

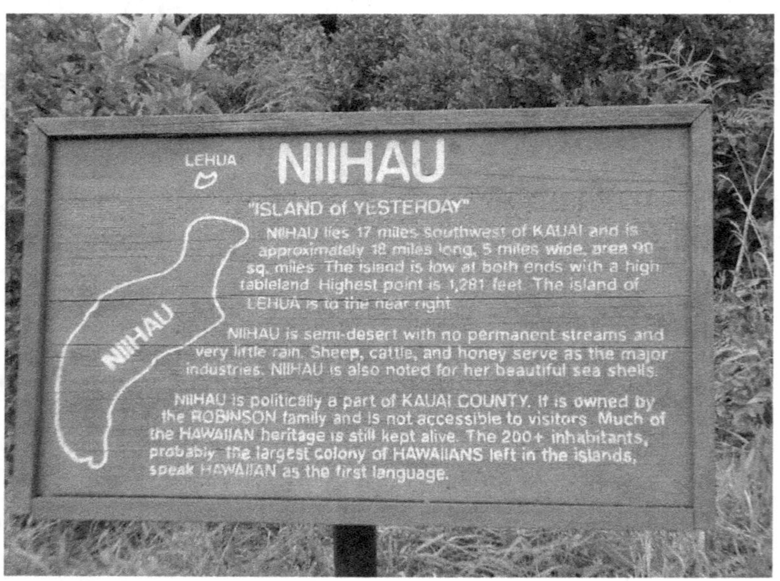

7-5-2017: (WH):

Re: NK / Niihau

North Korea likes to play tough because it makes them look admirable or important, as they are a minor threat. Giving them attention spurs them on. If you feel threatened by them, why not prevent the components of their missiles from entering their country? Unless they make everything themselves, it has to come from somewhere. Then starve them like *Alexander the Great* (**M7**) did to the City of Tyre; when they want aid, trade aid for nukes.

Also, I believe **the residents on Niihau Island need compensation** for living in substandard conditions. Use UEIR Funds or revenue from UEIR Taxes (M7 Estate) **to pay each Native/Resident $100,000 per month.** Importing Water is expensive. They can use water for farming, sanitation and living. Thank you. (**Niihau Pharaocracy Founding Day is July 5, 2000**). M7-2017.

https://en.wikipedia.org/wiki/Kahoolawe

https://en.wikipedia.org/wiki/Lanai

https://en.wikipedia.org/wiki/Niihau

Note:

Because of M7's classification any "Government secrets" about M7's assets is not public. **The public profile of Niihau**, for example, **does not mention M7** or the *Pharaocracy of Niihau.* So no one will find anything linking Niihau with M7 in public records. Such secrets were unlawfully acquired by an Arab Family once. This was illegal for them to do so. The information was made public via gossip and rumors *throughout* **Hawaii and California** from 2004-2017 CE. M7 does not possess any of this real estate **until** the Government either declassifies him, or compensates him.

Niihau = 71 Square Miles

Lanai = 141 Square Miles

Kahoolawe = 45 Square Miles

Molokai = 260 sq. miles.

(517+ Sq. Miles) – not including others.

Copyright © M7 2017.

Long ago, when the land was barren and without plants, the Creator came to this World. He was alone. In his loneliness, he wept. His tears formed the Oceans. Then a thought of inspiration occurred to him, so he spat into the Oceans, and a plant poked out from the Seas. The plant opened up a flower, in the form of a blue Lotus blossom. The flower opened up and the Sun appeared from within. The Sun was called **Ra.** The scent of the flower was the Air, called **Amon.** The Creator called himself **Ptah** because he spat into the Oceans. The names of everything also came from him.

Out from the Seas some land erupted below as a volcano. This was Pele, Goddess of Fire. Her hair formed lava rock, and her eyes gave life to the islands. Ptah mated with Pele, and their offspring was the **Akua** named Mika'ele, or "**M7.**" The Akua M7 became King of the Islands, as he ruled with Mana (Energy or Power). This Mana came from Ra. Akua M7 ruled with balance and intelligence; his ideas shaped society. Then Akua M7 left the islands and made a promise to return some day.

Ptah and Akua M7 voyaged East and founded a Country called *Kemet*, which is the native word for **Egypt**, which meant *House of the Spirit of Ptah* in Ancient Greek. Akua M7 created civilization in Egypt and these ideas spread everywhere he traveled. The Egyptians developed a form of writing involving pictures; this was also given to the Islands. Ptah then created the Heavens as a place to retire to after Earthly life. Akua M7 would visit this place in between visits to this World.

Later, Akua M7 traveled from Egypt across the Atlantic Ocean, up to Central America where he founded the Toltec Civilization. He was called **Quetzalcoatl** among the Toltecs, and he made the same promise to return in the future, to examine their progress and commitment to Civilization.

Akua M7 returned to Egypt many times, then once he returned after the Romans took possession of Egypt. Akua M7 became known as the Christ, which in Egypt was called QRST, a word meaning "Burial in a tomb." His followers were called Christians, and he made a promise to return in the future, which he *always* honored via **reincarnation**.

Akua M7 returned to the islands and gave them civilization from **ideas** he gained while in Egypt. He gave them knowledge of how to make Bark Cloth for clothing and sails, Egyptian tools like the Adze, and feathery costumes to wear in ceremonies. He taught farming and fishing techniques. He taught Magic and rituals, and writing in the form of petro-glyphs (based on Egyptian writing or Hieroglyphs).

Hawaii was united by conquest and made into a Kingdom. These islands were part of the islands created by Pele and Ptah, to be ruled by Akua M7 in the distant future. In the future life, Akua M7 returned to Hawaii. He conquered 2 Superpowers or great nations with his Mana, and instilled civilization and set taxes. With the taxes he purchased **Niihau, Lanai, and Kahoolawe** from one Superpower which owned the islands of Hawaii as one of its States. This Superpower was called America, and it was founded by members of Akua M7's Egyptian descendants, called *Freemasons*. The Great Seal shows Akua M7's **birthright** to rule the World, with the Egyptian Pyramid and American-Egyptian symbol of Horus-Ra. For in Egypt, Akua M7 was a Pharaoh.

Akua M7 founded his New Hawaiian Kingdom called *Akua Niihau Pharaocracy.* It will be populated and governed by Native Hawaiians *when possible* under the framework of Pharaoh, Akua M7. At least one town will resemble Ancient Egyptian architecture. Native Hawaiians did not have much in the way of Architecture besides stone temples and grassy or thatched ceilings.

Akua M7 used his Mana to guide and restore Civilization when necessary, to fight injustice, to destroy evil, influence Nature, create Peace and support the economy, and other ideas via his divine intervention. He may return in the Future if he desires to. **His full name and titles are:** *(Pharaoh) Horus M7, Akua Mika'ele, beloved of Ptah-Amon-Ra, beloved of Pele and Ptah, righteous one of Ku & Kane, first among equals, honored of Lono, the Akua of the Alii, Master of Time, and Protector of the Islands / Guardian of Kemet.*

Niihau Kahelelani "Royal" Shells

M7's Hotel: Formerly the *Westin Kauai.*

Chapter 9:

UEIR as USA

Why does USA resemble the UEIR?

1. USA was founded by Freemasons, the secret society of the UEIR in 1776.
2. Freemasons are descended from the architects of Egyptian Pharaohs and Priests.
3. Egypt was 2 States united by Pharaoh.
4. The White House (i.e. Palace, Pharaoh) has an Oval Office (a Cartouche) to protect the President.
5. The Washington Monument is an Egyptian Obelisk. Obelisks attract evil energy from the ground and pull it into the sky where it is destroyed when sunlight hits the pyramid on top.
6. The Great Seal of USA has a Pyramid on one side and a Ra-Horus Eagle on the other, with solar crown as 13 stars similar to the Star of David.
7. The Capitol building has pillars and bronze statues of its leaders.
8. In the Civil War, the North conquered the South (Horus conquered Set); both USA and Egypt had slaves once.
9. There are 12 signs of the Zodiac plus the Sun to make 13. The same is with Christ with his 12 Apostles.

10.   The US Constitution was written on paper, not stone, so it should be corrected. Yet the authors refused so they attached amendments that can be revoked later.

11.   The Pledge of Allegiance to the Flag of the United States of America – the flag was the symbol for Deity in Egypt, and placing one's hand over their heart is a salute to the Sun God Ra. Liberty and Justice is called Ma'at. One Nation under God = one nation under Ra.

12.   Trial by Jury is like the Court of Osiris with 42 "separate judges" as a Jury separate from "supreme judge Osiris." Anubis is the Lawyer, and Thoth is the Recorder.

13.   Presidential term limits are the Heb-Sed Festival of Pharaoh, or Jubilee, where Pharaoh is tested for fitness to govern every 15 to 30 years.

14.   USA has counties separate from cities. In Egypt these are called Nomes.

15.   The Pentagon holds a 5 point star; the symbol for Duat is a 5 pointed star in a circle, like in USA Police badges.

16.   The word President was a title in Ancient Egypt.

17.   Elections are mock battles, which represent the battles of Horus/Set for control of Egypt before Osiris.

18.	Both (Ancient) Egypt and USA are cosmopolitan and materialistic cultures.

19.	The Lincoln memorial resembles an Egyptian Temple.

20.	There are gold-plated statues in Washington D.C. as in Egypt.

21.	In USA there are freeways for travel, in Egypt canals connected to the Nile River as freeways.

22.	The USA Flag has stars and stripes; an Egyptian Pharaoh wore a striped Nemes cloth head dress, and stars on a cloak.

23.	The bird on the flag pole is an Eagle; in Egypt this is Horus on the standard carried into battle. Flags were positioned near Temples, and are symbols for Deity (NTR).

24.	The God Osiris is more Democratic than a Monarch, especially when funerary ceremonies in the New Kingdom were allowed for common people.

25.	Presidents were represented in profile on currency to prevent being attacked on their front when pressed upon by malicious citizens.

26.	Napoleon Bonaparte invaded Egypt because of the Freemasons' new society in USA (for knowledge), and to acquire magical stones for world conquest.

27.   Napoleon sold the Louisiana Purchase to USA fearing Britain would acquire it, and to later colonize it if he was ever exiled to USA, as he was to Elba. This didn't happen. His Code Napoleon is still Law in New Orleans.

28.   Lady Liberty is female as is the Egyptian goddess Ma'at.

29.   The statue of Liberty is a colossus statue in USA; similar to Ramses the Great's statues.

30.   George Washington was buried in a brick tomb, similar to Egyptian tombs.

31.   Buildings in Washington D.C. look like Egyptian or Roman Temples.

32.   Capitalism is similar to Egyptian Feudalism, with workers wearing a business tie (slaves' yoke), and work for companies (groups), with the majority of profit going to the Government (Pharaoh).

33.   Both countries had complex Tax systems based on profit.

34.   US States have a patron animal or goddess (Athena in California) or flower. Egypt had animal totems and State Flowers.

35.   USA flags and Egyptian standards were carried into battle. Both had cloth flags for noticing the wind, and birds on top.

36.	In USA the Church is separate from the State, but in Egypt both are combined into the Pharaoh with Priests as advisers.

37.	Pharaohs also led the Military in Egypt; Presidents are Commander in Chief of the Military.

38.	Pharaohs had ceremonial roles; Presidents have similar roles for awards ceremonies, dedications, or buildings.

39.	Pharaohs awarded "gold flies" for valor, and Golden Collars for achievement; Presidents award Medals of Freedom or Citizenship.

40.	Egyptian Citizens were not slaves, so they were Free or had freedoms.

41.	American Presidents can be dynastic (Roosevelt, Bush, Adams) as were Egyptian Pharaohs.

42.	Most American Presidents and Egyptian Pharaohs were male.

43.	Both Egypt and USA had African Slaves.

44.	Both Pharaohs and Presidents are under oath in coronation ceremonies.

45.	The Egyptian afterlife was "to the west" of Egypt; America is a western nation.

46.	Both Egypt and USA had gold mines, vineyards, a Navy, an Army, and Science in some form.

47.   Both Egypt and USA had an "Alexandria" and named places after people.

UEIR = United Egyptian Imperial-Republic.

Chapter 10:

Maps:

Niihau, Kahoolawe, & Lanai

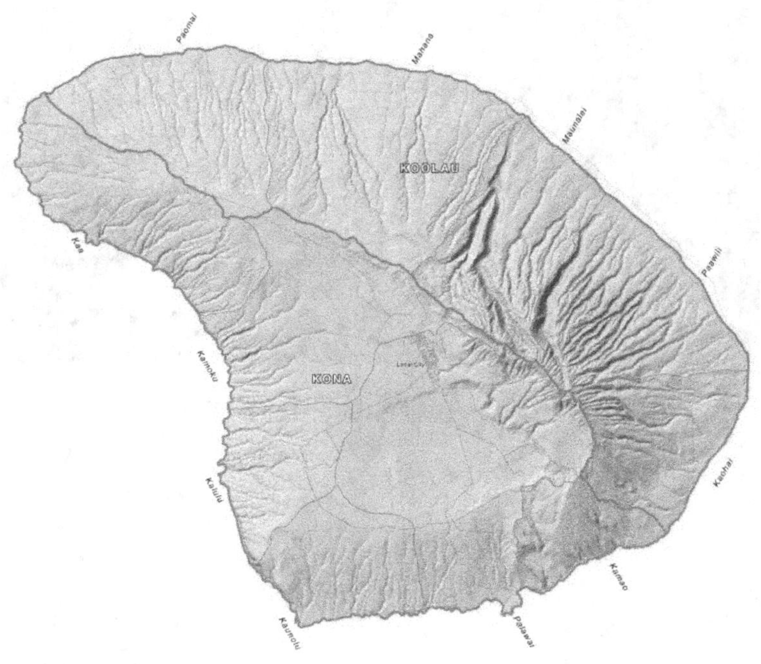

Lanai Island (2015 CE)

Niihau Island (2000 CE)

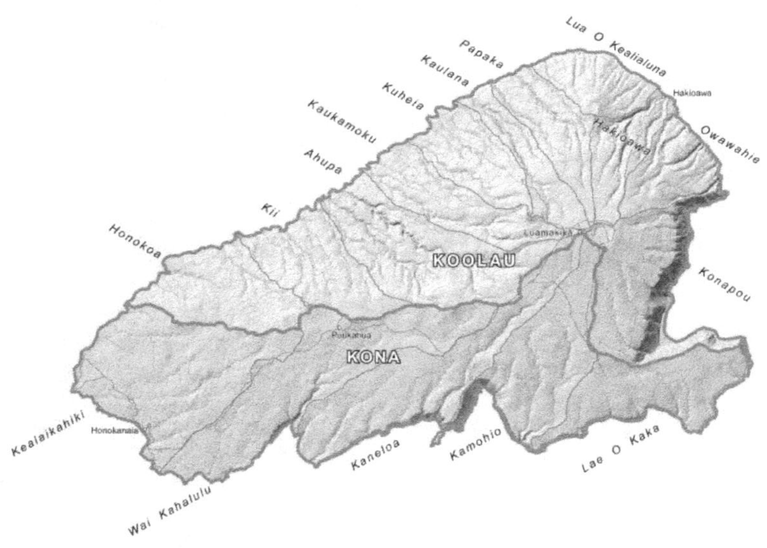

Kahoolawe Island (2016 CE)

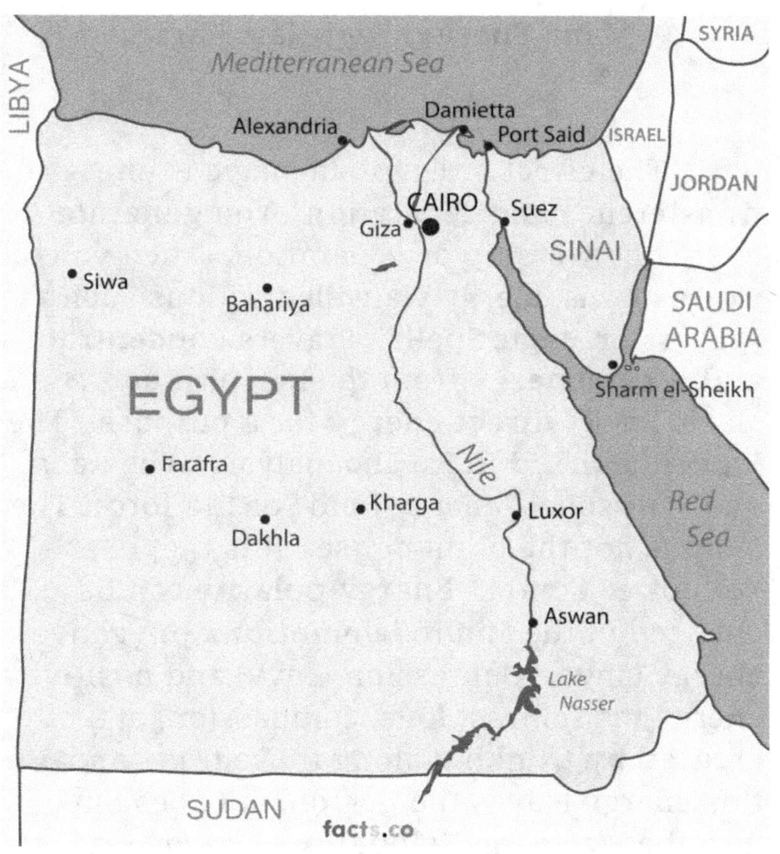

Egypt (UEIR), (2016 CE)

Chapter 11:

Mana Energy, Egyptian Magic:

The effect of Egyptian Magic is **energy** transference and generation. You **generate** energy by worship or veneration. Then you **express** this energy via willed actions such as prayers or Magic Spells. Prayers **concentrate and focus energy** from the Ka Spirit and Mind. Magic Spells **direct energy** for a purpose. The **Ka** is like the **Id** in Psychoanalysis. The Ka is one's personal "energy field" or life force. The Mind is not the brain per se. It is the Willpower Center. **Energy polarity** can be changed in the Mind **via emotions** – negative energy (anger, depression, envy) and positive energy (happiness, love, compassion) are **created by thinking** along those traits and this energy leaves the person and goes out into the World via **Telepathy**. The energy comes into contact with living people or animals and causes events related to that polarity – negative energy makes people angry or hostile, positive energy makes people happy or caring or fortunate. Energy also affects the Earth & Weather.

Other cultures have experienced this **energy**. Hawaiian culture calls it "Mana" or spiritual energy. Chinese call it "Chi" energy. In Egypt it is "Sakhem" or power. It primarily is developed in the Sun as noticed in the **Tropics or Equator**. Ra the solar Deity of Egypt is the "Father of Magic," and Sun worship was the key feature of the Pyramid Age. Cultures near the Tropics tend to have Polytheism – the more energy you have, the more Gods exist there. Pyramids exist in Central America and Egypt from Solar Worship.

To acquire energy naturally is simple: go get some **sunlight**. This also helps reduce a form of Depression during Winter and gives you Vitamin D.

Egyptian Deities are effective in Magic Spells. Though they **must be appeased** in order to use their sacred names correctly (not angry) **or the opposite effect** results. A story or mythology can accompany the Deity. The story helps focus energy from Believing; the **act of believing** is a mental action that **channels energy** from the Mind. The **story** of *Jesus Christ* helps people pray, whether or not if it is accurate or even real. By saying it is not real **attacks one's ability to believe** or focus energy. So you may have a religion and still practice Egyptian Magic.

Queen Hatshepsut made a mythology for herself as *"Daughter of Amon."* *Akhenaton* made a mythology for his new God *the Aton* (Sun). *Cleopatra 7* created a mythology about the Goddess Isis.

To worship (generate energy) Egyptian Deities:

1. Flattery
2. Daily or Weekly Offerings
3. (Burn) Fragrant Incense, Flowers
4. Stories or Myths
5. Build Temples, statues, artwork
6. Personal Righteous Conduct (Ma'at)
7. Preserve Civilization

To activate the energy:

1. Call the Deity's name
2. Place a bookmark touching the Spell
3. Write a Poem or Spell about them
4. Mentally focus on their identity
5. Repeat the name several times a day
6. Repeat the spell or prayer
7. Wait for effect once done

Acknowledging the effect or removing a **bookmark** that was touching the Spell usually **ends the action**.

Ideas that interfere with the ability to concentrate are: causing Doubts and rejection, inability to believe, distractions, random thoughts, psychic attacks, Anxiety, etc. This is remedied by Meditation techniques, exercising (physically or mentally), incense, peace of mind, or neutral thoughts. Excessive prayers cause Telepathy, and Natural Telepathy is known to be Genetic.

The Weather is controlled by gravity and energy. Solar and Lunar activities influence the tides, animals and plants, and their behavior. Storms, quakes, and droughts are affected by energy. These are manipulated from the ground by Telepaths. The Sun is affected by Sun worship from Earth, causing solar storms, flares, etc. **Gods who are incarnate** have greater effect than humans who try to use Egyptian Magic; their Magic is usually more advanced or better than standard. Incarnate Gods have this nocturnal fiery **emerald light** inside them, like an **Aura**. Externally it resembles a green fireball or a "Burning Bush" (Exodus myth, OT, Bible).

Energy may be summoned to you, though most attraction spells **need 1 week** in advance for activity.

Offerings traditionally followed **an invocation list**. In the **Pyramid Age** this was "a loaf of bread, a jar of beer, and a jar of incense." In **New Kingdom** era, it was enlarged to "1000 of bread, beer, fowl, oxen (meat), wine, linen, alabaster (stone vessels), perfume, incense, etc." Murals show Egyptians placing pots of water, oil, milk, wine, etc. in tombs for the Gods as offerings. Or they placed offerings on small tables made of Papyrus reeds. Written offerings *sometimes* replaced physical ones.

Offerings are compensation for an action if an Egyptian Deity is asked to do something. Money is not always offered, but is accepted, along with real estate for Temple construction or farming. Internet "website" **Temples** is a modern form of worship. Egyptian Deities are spiritual so they can see everything occurring on Earth *when alerted to it*. Otherwise they sleep in Duat. Preserving Civilization and **upholding Ma'at** by righteous conduct / civil behavior is a substitute for offerings. Compliments on a Deity are flattery, unlike Demons who don't appreciate anything positive. **Flattery** is positive comments, descriptions, compliments, that make them feel welcome or esteemed.

Incense sends messages to Heaven, clears the air from negativity, freshens a room, removes bad scents like waste, animal dung, or decay. It is helpful for Meditation and calming or breathing exercises. Fragrant incense can be purchased in stores or online, in stick form, cones, powder, or natural resin. It is burnt with a flame (from a lighter or candle), and sends the smoke upwards. Flowers or perfumed oils are a common substitute if burning is not allowed.

Advice:

Always write your name in a Cartouche when practicing Egyptian Magic (even when not royal). This is the "Magic Circle" (see *The White House* in Washington DC; **"Oval Office"**).

The Cartouche is 2D (Two Dimensional) so when enemies use written spells, which are usually 2D, the words cannot harm anything written in the closed oval. You can include other elements like pets, your home, friends or family, with the name.

Cast Protection Spells first BEFORE Counter Magic. Protect yourself in case of redirected energy. The Earth is a sphere, so anything sent in one direction will *eventually* return to its source (i.e. You).

If a spell doesn't work as desired DO NOT insult the Deity for it, or future spells may be delayed if using that Deity. Not everyone reads your handwriting perfectly.

DO NOT cast spells just to see "if it works," because all spells have the capacity to work, and you don't need to have a guilty conscience should you cause Natural Disasters. Only cast whatever is needed or wanted, not unwanted or unnecessary. This wastes energy. Not all spells work as expected all the time.

DO NOT overload the Magic Spell book! Too many active spells causes problems. Remove bookmarks if not vital to the situation. 10 active spells are estimated maximum per week, or as many as you can handle once proficient.

Record results in a paper notebook for reference. Add date when Spell was cast and date when it worked. Record velocity of weather or earthquake or any damage; also record any unusual dreams involving Egyptian Deities.

Use photos of targets in Magic Spell book, either for healing or counter Magic. Remove when not active.

DO NOT fight evil with more evil. This only contributes to more negative energy. And no one wants to be there when it returns. Fight Darkness with Solar Light. *Hail Ra!*

Be certain the chosen Deity is in a good mood to prevent opposite reactions. No one is returning your spell against you. ***Placate the Deity first, & then cast the spell. Or placate them after it is cast.*** Ahmose asked Amon to liberate Egypt from the Hyksos; in return he said he would make Amon into the Chief Deity of the Two Lands. Today, Karnak Temple of Amon-Ra is the largest in Egypt, and the Hyksos were removed. The Sphinx made a request to make a Prince into the Pharaoh only if he cleared the sand from his position; this promise was honored. The Gods honor their promises, unlike human governments.

Chapter Bibliography:

The Complete Gods and Goddesses of Ancient Egypt © Richard H. Wilkinson, 2003T&H

Magic in Ancient Egypt © Geraldine Pinch, 1994, University of Texas Press

Effective Egyptian Magic Spells 4 © Horus Michael, 2016.

Egyptian Magic: Be your own Kheriheb Priest © Horus Michael, 2017.

www.amazon.com/author/horusmichael

(The UEIR was classified top secret by CIA)

Energy Spells:

To acquire Magical energy to work the Spells:

SAKHMET   RA KHEPERI PTAH

To acquire Internet Wi-Fi connection:

NUT AMUN MAAT SOBEK

To restore energy during an outage or blackout:

AMONRA SAKHMET SERQET RA

To cause the Sun to appear from storm clouds:

ATON   RA PTAH HORUS

To restore an Internet connection:

PTAH KA AKH MAAT

To black out a power grid:

TUTANKHAMON APOPHIS NUN

To acquire Fuel for a vehicle:

ONURIS RA AMON

To cause wind power:

AMUN   SHU   PTAH

Protection Spells:

For protection of one's home, family, friends, pets, belongings, jobs, estate, city, and lifestyle **while traveling**:

BASTET NEPHTHYS SERQET ISIS NEITH

For protection while driving from other cars, accidents, texting/cell phone calls, road-kill, erosion, weather, reckless, speeding, etc.:

BES AMON HAROERIS SOBEK MAATI

For protection from (childhood) Bullies, Gangs, organized crime, robbers or thieves, arsonists or anarchists, rioters, terrorists, or **other criminals**:

HORUS ONURIS MAAT PTAH

For protection from Cyber Crimes (Internet, computer related), hackers, trolls, flamers, phishing, identity theft, etc.:

BES THOTH ANUBIS AMMOT IAH

For protection while giving birth:

BES TAURET NUT MUT NEFERTUM

Protection Spells:

For Protecting your City, State, or Country from terrorism and other crimes:

    HORUR OSIRIS MAAT ATUM

For protection from the Weather, erosion, storms, earthquakes, tsunamis, etc.:

    TEFNUT GEB SHU PTAH

For protection of Police and Soldiers:

    HORUS MAATI NEITH SOBEK

For protection from feral / wild animals:

    ANAT PATAIKOS BASTET BES

For protection from unstable people:

    WADJET MUT SET BES

For a Guardian Angel (Akhu/Akua):

    AKH-NEFRU PTAH ATUM NEITH

To find something that is missing or lost:

    THOTH SESHAT IMHOTEP NUT

Weather Spells:

To cause rain:

TEFNUT SIA IAH

To cure a drought (*warning:* lots of rain):

TEFNUT-AA SET

To cause some wind:

AMUN SHU

To cause a rainbow:

TEFNUT SHU

For warm air or climate:

SHU ATUM

For small earthquakes:

GEB SHU

For sunlight:

ATON RA SHU

For a storm:

TEFNUT SET SAKHMET

Medical or Healing:

To relieve sickness or cure diseases:

IMHOTEP IAH THOTH NU

To heal injuries and wounds:

ISIS MUT SESHET NUT

To heal (or cure) **Cancer:**

SAKHMET NEITH SERQET BES RA

To reduce Tumors:

SAKHMET IMHOTEP RA

To relieve common viruses or bacteria:

THOTH SET SERQET BES

To reduce Depression:

RA ATUM KHEPERI NEFERU

For excellent Health:

SAKHMET IMHOTEP NEFRU-SONEB

To meditate:

ATUM PTAH MERIT

Medical or Healing:

To heal the Liver:

IMSETY ISIS

To heal the Stomach:

DUAMUTEF NEITH

To heal the Lungs:

HAPY NEPHTHYS

To heal the Intestines and Colon:

QEBESENUEF SERQET

To heal insect stings:

SERQET BES

To heal Magical Energy effects:

SERQET NETRA ISIS NUT

To heal Mental Illness:

THOTH SESHET TEP-NEFRU SHAY

For visions, inspiration:

PTAH NEFERTUM SHAY MAAT

Financial or Prosperity:

For a good Harvest or **economic prosperity**:

AMONRA SHEZMU SHAY OSIRIS NEPER

To attract treasures, money, gems, art:

AMONRA NUB ATON ATUM

To find hidden treasures or buried treasure:

AMONRA NUB SHAY

To attract employment opportunities:

SHAY AMONRA NEPER PTAH

For protection from lawsuits or litigation:

SHAY MAAT ANUBIS AMON

For Good Luck, Positive Energy:

NEFERU-SAKHMET RA SHAY

For Success:

MAA-KHERU HORUS NEITH

For gold or silver:

NUB SHAY AMONRA RA-ATON

Counter Magic:

For defense, **to protect from negativity**:

SHAY NEFERU NUT

To deflect all curses sent against you:

SAKHMET NEPHTHYS ISIS HEKA

To change polarity of Magical Energy:

SET-HORUS SAKHEM NEFRU

For fertility:

MIN HATHOR NEFERTUM

To Undo any Magic whatsoever:

NI-HEKAU SHAY NEFERU

To Undo all curses and enchantment:

NI-HEKAU NI-SESHET MAAT

To prevent Sorcerers from operating:

HEKA NI-HEKAU ISIS BES

To prevent Magic from back-firing or inversion:

HEKA SHAY HEH NEFRU

Counter Magic:

To protect your neighborhood and City:

BES WEPWAWET INPUT MAAT

To attack your enemies with Magic:

SET HORUS NEITH KHERTY

To cause your enemies to become sick or injured or have **accidents**:

SHAY SET SAKHMET

To attack those who insult or attack you with words, written slander, gossip, rumors, etc.:

NI-THET-THET MAAT ATUM

To attack those **who spy on you** or collect your personal information, stalk, harass, gossip about or annoy:

KHNUM SOBEK NEPHTHYS SERQET

To attack those who give **low ratings** on your products (on websites or Internet):

SET HORUS AMMOT SOTHIS

<u>**Chapter 12: UEIR History:**</u>

The **mythical origins of the UEIR** occur in the Science Fiction Novel, *Eye of the Pharaoh* © 1990-1995 MJC, in *Chapter 20* after the fall of the "Arab Terrorist States" (Caliphate in 2014 CE). The actual Empire is under Pharaoh M7 of the real UEIR, a country based in the Egyptian Netherworld for safety. It is this country that is **being advertised by the USA Government** as part of its Covenant with the UEIR. The USA took **UEIR letterhead** and **made commercials** out of it. This started in 1993 CE and continues today (2017+).

Climate Change is part of Egyptian Weather Magic. The UEIR *overthrew* the USSR and *conquered* the USA **to end the Cold War**. This is better than being a shadow on a wall had nuclear war occurred. Since UEIR *founded* USA, there is no further revision needed. **Pharaoh M7** was President Kennedy & Lincoln previously.

The UEIR is a secret society of reincarnated and paranormal people mostly from Ancient Egypt. Citizens relocated to Duat during the Roman Empire, waiting to return. When Napoleon went to Egypt and opened the tombs of Egyptians and read their names, our people "awoke" and returned to Earth. Most of us are in North America, but some migrate back to Egypt.

Our origins date back to Dynastic Egypt because we wanted to retain souls from life in a secure place. These are people we met and would like to see again, as with family or friends. Landscape in Duat is based on Earth regions where souls depart from.

So we returned to Earth in between Ancient Egypt and Modern times, influencing other cultures like China, Europe, or Central America and Polynesia. Modern people tend to forget spiritual information and replace it with false theories and rigid Sciences. So we need to return to Earth to fix such issues and keep the system working.

Iapana Province was founded in CA in 1994, then the Kingdom of Niihau on July 5, 2000. Both are regions in UEIR/USA.

Following are **examples of reincarnation** and its effect on the next life as a UEIR Citizen.

Tutankhamon

Remembering **Reincarnated Memories** is a lot like finding a **pattern of actions** from one's current life and searching for its counterpart in the past. You need to study whatever you are currently doing **to find blocked memories**, because you are the same person, just in a new bodily form. **Real Reincarnation is more than just feelings** – "Oh I think I have some connection to Ancient Egypt because I love cats! I *must be* Cleopatra!" **Real Reincarnation is about a pattern of actions that lead to a repeat of History.** It's only that, YOUR HISTORY.   Even if you were not famous, you are not new here. Maybe if you are in a gang and spray paint your "tag" on a wall, you were a wolf or dog in a previous life (dogs urinate on walls to mark territory). Or if you use Twitter or like to sing or gossip, you were a bird. If you love swimming you were some aquatic animal or fish. If I encounter places or environments familiar to a past visit **I unblock memories**. This also works with **Artifacts** or photographs of Artifacts. Information **triggers** subconscious memory. This may lead to having a **vision** of sorts. It's like the new **Dalai Lama** - a child who must choose between numbers of artifacts connected to previous owners, to see which Dalai Lama the child may have been. This assumes the Dalai Lama is always human. This is not always correct because there is no spiritual **rest** in between lives.

My first "**past life**" I can remember happened in the 1970s via television and a dream the previous night. The dream was about a girl dressed in 18th Dynasty clothing in a flowering garden. The girl had short black hair and bronze skin with cobalt blue eyes. She was very pretty. The next day I was alerted to the televised **Tutankhamon Tour** in San Francisco, CA at the **De Young Museum**. I was literally glued to the television. When we traveled towards the museum on the Bay Bridge, I would acquire feelings of "ancient familiarity" like visiting one's previous home. This stopped when the tour moved onto other cities. The same effect happened when I first visited the **Rosicrucian Egyptian Museum** in San Jose, CA in the 1980s. I bought a copy of the Egyptian funerary text there. I even wrote my own starting in 1994. The girl in the dream would visit me in other dreams and in other ways. I believe the girl is **Ankhesenamon**. I tried looking for a human counterpart on Earth but only found false leads. So it must be her. When I read

Egyptology books I can sometimes "feel data" which enables new theories that unblock information. That there is a plethora of ideas about Tutankhamon is expected in the Egyptology community – everyone wants fame. Some want **to be** Tutankhamon. If only they knew that is a bad idea.

On the topic of life and death I remember telling (my mother at the time) Queen **Cleopatra VII** when I was **Ptolemy Caesar** (Caesarion or "Little Caesar") about how I died when I was Tutankhamon. Tut was known by a reference in the Alexandrian Library. I told her I "dressed up in my royal attire and committed suicide in the 'traditional royal manner' via an **Asp cobra snake**." The Asp was a "pet cobra" of Tutankhamon, and is very deadly and poisonous. When Cleopatra remembered her life as "**Maat-ka-nefer**" (daughter of Menkaura of 4th Dynasty) she died the same way. So perhaps she perfected the role? History believes so.

Current data on Tutankhamon is that he "died within a day of breaking his left leg" and that his body "appeared burned" but whether this is a chemical reaction to perfumed oils on his mummy or a fire that broke out in the original tomb is currently unknown. He had a Malaria Fever in his system, but this could be his immunity to the disease. The sarcophagus he was found in was yellow quartzite painted pinkish to resemble the broken red granite lid that went with a smaller red granite sarcophagus, like the one in **King Ay's tomb** in WV23. The lid was repaired in ancient times but the matching sarcophagus was repaired in modern times. **People believed King Ay's tomb was originally for Tutankhamon however I believe that Tutankhamon *faked his own death* and *became* King Ay.** This has to do with the "letters sent by an Egyptian Queen to the Hittite King asking him for a son to marry and become Pharaoh of Egypt."

The letters were written by Ankhesenamon because she wanted to contribute to the political world and be a teammate with her husband (Female Queens wanted to share the Government with their husband), or that she suspected infidelity or wanted to resolve the political issue with the Hittites' invasion of Syria. Tut found the Egyptian **copy** of these letters on the person of **Vizier Ay**. The Plague or epidemic that ravaged Akhetaton city was almost contained; it killed most of his family. Tut ordered General / Heir to the Throne / Crown Prince Horemhab to "visit the Hittites." The Hittite Prince may have been captured on the way to Egypt. The Plague visited the Hittites, too.

The letters said Tut "died." So the World knew this. Tut imprisoned Vizier Ay (or killed him) and impersonated him until Horemhab returned, then committed suicide via Asp. "King Ay" was persecuted by Horemhab, thinking it was Vizier Ay. Tut's tomb was violated in WV23 by Horemhab (or "King Ay" tomb) and was moved back to KV62, as the last time KV62 was opened was under Horemhab 's reign. Tut remained married to Ankhesenamon as King Ay, and the **mural in KV62** is actually self-serving. **Tut's face is on King Ay's body performing last rites to his former self.**

The age of **Tut's mummy** was originally believed to be **25 or so years old**, but wine casks in the tomb dated to year 10 which would be age 19. **If he ruled as King Ay and died at 19, then he started at age 5, ruled as Tut until 15, then "died and became King Ay" for 4 years until committing suicide by Asp at 19.** King Pepi became King at age 5, for example. His mummy is damaged from cut marks (either from when Howard Carter tried removing the gold mask and other relics, or from Ancient Violators who cut open the mummy looking for treasure. If this was done by error from Horemhab for Ay's persecution – *lo and behold it's actually Tutankhamon and not Vizier Ay* – Tut was reburied in

Ankhesenamon's tomb in KV62). **Why was Ankhesenamon buried in KV62?** The tomb is meant for a female based on design. The Canopic shrine has statues resembling her, and Canopic Jar stoppers without the false-beard, ideally feminine. The yellow quartzite sarcophagus is hers and re-cut for Tut. Most of the tomb items are from her. Perhaps she is buried behind the mural? (See my book *"KV62B the search for the resting place of Queen Ankh-kheperura (Ankhesenamon)"* on Amazon.com).

My first novel was about Tutankhamon. It was stolen when I was 19 (1991) and published on the open market. I also "faked my death" after telling the world about this situation in 1994, about the time Tut did that 3300 years ago. It was published by a woman who knew about my childhood, and she was the **reincarnated Priestess of Osiris** who was one of Tut's admirers. The Priestess listened to Tut tell her about his previous lives in Egypt. He gave her a tour of Egypt, pointing out all the places he remembered – Menkaura, Thutmose 3, Amonhotep 3, etc. She once tried to kiss him in Hatshepsut's valley Temple. They even once mated in her Nile side apartment. **Ankhesenamon** discovered this treasonous affair, and they had a fight about it, and she wrote letters to the Hittites in revenge. The Priestess saw Tut as King Ay, and believed Tut was indeed Osiris – the Egyptian King who **resurrected**. She started a gossip or rumor about this, which is why Tut committed suicide. The woman who published my book was my **babysitter in 1975**. I was sleeping on her floor once and she didn't see me there when she walked on my head, and I died. I awoke in Duat (Egyptian Netherworld). I returned to my body and (there were no witnesses) **resurrected** via a burst of energy which went up her spine, curing her of partial deafness and other ailments. She became nervous and went to get her camera, taking 3 black and white photos. When my Mother returned for me 10 minutes later, the babysitter blurted out "I stepped on him", but my Mother didn't hear it. The woman told me this in 1994 and **via unblocked memories**. The woman was studying to be a Psychologist. I told her I was Tutankhamon **reborn**. You get the idea. Much gossip resulted from this situation up to this day.

The *Opening of the Mouth Ceremony* was performed by the **last male heir** to the King. Ay wasn't. But since Horemhab was not there, someone had to fill this position. And because Ay was the "servant" that Ankhesenamon didn't want to marry, as the mail courier, Tut chose to be King Ay. The ceremony is performed by a KheriHeb Priest. There is equipment for a **KheriHeb Priest** in the tomb of Tut. Tutankhamon as a Pharaoh would not need this. But if Tut was also a KheriHeb Priest **and** Pharaoh, perhaps he would. In Ancient Egypt one could have multiple occupations. **He used Magic to conquer his enemies**. Since he was not physically able to be a normal warrior, Magic replaced this condition. In my current life I am a KheriHeb Priest (since 1980s) and a Micronation Pharaoh. I also use Egyptian Magic to conquer countries. The Messiah is a Priest and a King, in case this helps.

When Tutankhamon was crowned he was 9 or almost 10 years old; when I was 9 going on 10 I moved to a new city. About 2 to 3 years later, Tut changed his name and government away from the Atonist regime; when I was 12 to 13 I had major Chest surgery, where I asked "Anubis to insert a heart scarab amulet." I started to notice that I could mentally influence the Weather via my emotions.

When Tut was first crowned I had this memory of "Here I go again" thoughts, because this wasn't the first time he was Pharaoh. In my current life, the same idea happened in my 7 to 9 years of age while walking home from school. I once imagined my enemy or school bully to be attacked by a bow and arrows; Tut was comfortable with Archery equipment. When I first held a bow during Junior College years, I hit a Bull's eye (holding the bow at a 45 degree angle). I later placed political enemies on Archery target faces (Iraq's Saddam Hussein during the first Iraq war in 1991. This was Psi Archery or Magical Warfare). Previously I used the Iranian Ayatollah for a dartboard target face; he died within 1 week of that. Tut may have written texts to foreign leaders laced with Chronokinesis Energy; now I can write letters in a future tense of Chronokinetic Energy and cause events. This is known to the CIA.

When I was younger I had to write a reelection speech as Pres Carter of USA for a class assignment. Carter had started the Peace among Egypt and Israel. If he remained President perhaps other events more positive would result. I failed the assignment, and Egyptian President Anwar al-Sadat was assassinated shortly thereafter as punishment from the Egyptian Gods. The Republican Party took over the White House with Reagan and later Bush Sr. In one class I was asked to write to Reagan about his use of Jelly Belly candy, using handwriting samples. No one teaches handwriting now. This started a trend. I could write to the Government and cause events upon them reading it, like Magic. I used an Alias for this.

There is no "Curse" of Tutankhamon – that is his **angry Ka Spirit** waking up and attacking the living **with hostile energy** whenever his name is called. If your mummy was violated and tomb destroyed you would be upset too. This usually stops when he goes back to sleep in his sarcophagus. It also causes Weather anomalies. Go watch the ending of "*Raiders of the Lost Ark.*"

When I first visited the Tour of Tutankhamon in Los Angeles, CA in 2005 there was nothing unusual or paranormal. In 2009 I was trapped in the De Young Museum gift shop for 1 hour *before* the exhibit, and the Antennae in San Francisco stopped working for hours. This was because Egyptologists awoke Tut in 2008 to do Genetic sampling. In 2009 I sent a copy of my book, **Tutianity**, to a College Professor. By late 2010 he died of Natural Causes after his son died from alcoholism related conditions; he once told me he was "King Ay." That's Vizier Ay becoming King *before* Tut discovered this plot. Nakhtmin was Ay's son. Both are missing their mummy. By January 2011, one week *after* Egyptologist Dr. Zahi Hawass said his intentions to "find Queen Ankhesenamon's tomb in Egypt" the **Arab Spring Revolution** happened. This was also attributed to cleaning Tut's silver war trumpet in the Cairo Museum.

As a child my parents argued. Tutankhamon's parents were no different. Much of what happened in Akhetaton **occurred behind closed doors**. So I can't remember details. I do know riots occurred in the later years of Akhenaton's reign. This may even have started a Civil War on religion. Today we have "Islamic" terrorism as a global war. Islamic groups represent the same type of twisted Monotheism that Akhenaton was spreading, going about and destroying religious relics. His New City was built on forced labor, even by young people. The majority of recruits in the Islamic groups are young people.

Akhenaton was probably **not** Tutankhamon's real father. When I was 2 or so my biological father left, and so my Mother had to remarry. Akhenaton adopted Tut as his "bodily heir." There is a name recorded that said "Tut-ankh**u**-aton was Akhenaton's son." The added "U" **infers** a twin brother. How many times was Tut's name changed? My step-father was descended from European royalty.

Akhenaton co-ruled with his daughters after **divorcing** Nefertiti. This includes Merit-aton and Ankhesenamon (as Ankhkheperura Neferneferuaton); Ankh absorbed her mother's titles. Then Ankh built her tomb in KV62 where she was later buried after Tut *became* King Ay. **Perhaps she is still there?**

In July 2017 Dr. Zahi "Khufu" Hawass said he discovered a tomb near King Ay's tomb and said it was **Ankhesenamon's tomb** or burial chamber. They used radar to find it. He said this with KV63/KV64 previously. YL21 Mummy was said to be hers as based on Genetic data. The two still born fetuses buried with Tut are **a similar situation** as the two still born offspring of JFK buried near his gravesite in Arlington Cemetery in Washington D.C. *Reincarnated People tend to repeat their past actions as evidence of rebirth.*

Ptolemy Caesar (Caesarion)

Because Julius Caesar did not heed warnings on his pending death, he had to reincarnate into his biological son, Ptolemy Caesarion. Ptolemy was born in Egypt. He once visited Rome with his cousin Octavian. This was while his mother Cleopatra was with Caesar. She was his mistress and political consort. After Caesar died, Cleopatra had to regularly seduce important politicians in her Palace in Alexandria, Egypt, for political gain or information. This stopped once she met Marc Antony. They had 2 sons and a daughter (Selene). Selene chided Ptolemy, calling him "Little Caesar" as an insult. His name meant "the lesser Caesar" not necessarily having to do with height.

Ptolemy built monuments in Egypt. He was tutored by a scholar when traveling. At the Battle of Actium, Marc Antony said to Cleopatra not to allow her son to travel with them because "it was too dangerous." Perchance this is why they lost? After Marc Antony killed himself upon losing this battle, Cleopatra locked herself in her Palace. She gave Ptolemy a large sum of gold and silver or "his inheritance" and told him to travel to India with his tutor.

On the way to India, his tutor betrayed him (**and took the map**), so Ptolemy walked back to Egypt. He heard of his mother's suicide and stayed in her Temple. Octavian was overheard by Selene talking about what to do with Ptolemy Caesar. Selene sought out Ptolemy in the Temple. She had him tied and bound by a guard, then attacked him (stomped him into unconsciousness; he later awoke and was walking in the darkness when someone came up from behind and killed him via strangulation or something). The Temple may have been in Upper Egypt or Alexandria (as the **map** was missing I do not remember where exactly he was).

Ptolemy wanted to marry **Livia** (Octavian's future wife) because she knew him in a past life, but couldn't. This was revealed to me by a Clairvoyant in 1980s. Most of the guards in Egypt were Nubian.

Alexander (the Great):

Alexander was the son of **Philip and Olympias** of Macedon (not Zeus). She told her son he was special and a son of Zeus. He spent his adulthood trying to verify this. Zeus was the King of the Gods in Greece. Alexander's parents also argued. His mother may have had a role in Philip's assassination, though blame was placed on Persia. And so like Horus avenging Osiris, Alexander went on his quest to avenge his parent's death.

I remember riding a horse in thick grassy fields. Alexander believed his childhood stories were real people, so his acceptance of the Armor of Achilles at the City of Troy was important to his belief system. Alexander drank watered-down wine or "Water Wine" a form of soft drink in Greece. Real wine made him sick. Greeks did not believe in Germs. When Alexander's best friend **Hephaestion** died of a Fever in Asia, Alexander was all over his corpse and contracted the same Fever that later killed them. He was not murdered or anything. Although he tried to create a makeshift pistol to open his cranium, it didn't work. **Ancient Greek Medicine said** *opening the cranium will release the heat.*

Much of his "glorious history" (Alexander Romance stories) was invented for theater purposes. A future incarnation was **Caligula Caesar**, whom wore the Armor of Alexander from his tomb in Alexandria, Egypt. Even **Julius Caesar** was witnessed crying after reading about his past life as Alexander, so he torched the Library of Alexandria (or the "accident" when Cleopatra heard of this). Marc Antony compensated "200,000 scrolls to the Library" when he was with Cleopatra. A distant future life was **Napoleon Bonaparte** who relived Caesar when in Gaul (**France**), and Alexander when marching in the snow back to France from Russia.

Hephaestion once approached Alexander as he was fantasizing about Amazons and started licking him to snap him out of it. He was dressed like an Amazon warrior. This was the "Meeting with the **Amazon Queen**" legend. One of his Generals said "We need to get Alexander a wife." This was before any girl friends existed in his all-male Army. Alexander **later married Roxanne** when he was in Persian country. I remember once asking her to make love while wearing armor in the bedroom. He used his sword to cut the "wedding cake." She had dark hair and eyes, as does her sister and cousins.

Chapter 13: Native Government

If in the event Pharaoh M7has no heirs or relatives to inherit this Government, or for other reasons, the **Kingdom of Niihau** will be governed by Native Hawaiians, Polynesians, or distant heirs of Native Hawaiian culture. Once Climate Change reverses from its current path and once ocean levels return to "normal" and not flood the coasts of California and Hawaii or other islands in danger of rising sea levels, the Government of Native Hawaiians should exist, in place of being elsewhere as it is at present. Otherwise it may be ruled by Duat (*Egyptian Netherworld*) and Pharaohs in Duat, **or become a Native Hawaiian theme park**.

Natives shall be educated in preserving their inherent culture as part of this park. **Admission prices** for visiting the islands, Museums, Libraries, Cultural Centers, Art Galleries, Colleges, Temples (both Hawaiian and Ancient Egyptian – if any), Stores, and Palaces **shall pay for its maintenance**. A membership club or organization shall help protect and maintain this property.

About the Author:

Horus Michael follows the training of Ancient Egyptian Priests in his varied works on the Occult. He also studies Egyptian Archaeology. He currently lives in California, USA.

www.amazon.com/author/horusmichael

www.amazon.com/author/michaeljcosta

@HorusMichaelM7

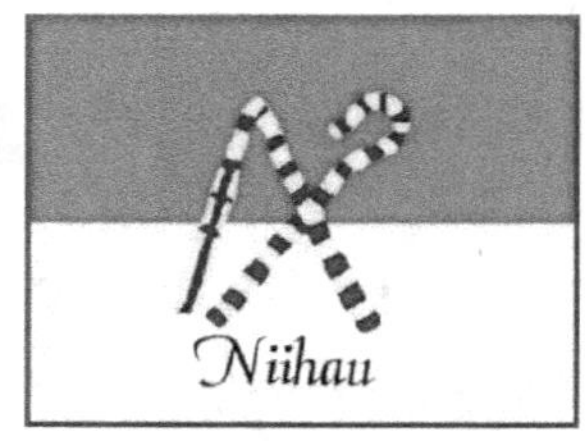

Instant Country, Just Add People!

Niihau * Lanai * Kahoolawe * UEIR

This is a Recognized Micronation virtually located on the Hawaiian Islands of Niihau, Lanai, and Kahoolawe. A recognized Micronation is a Sovereign State according to the United Nations. To be recognized is simple: have a real country, like the USA, acknowledge a Micronation and communicate with it, such as commercially advertise it via Mass Media. A Micronation is an independent or new country, typically not official due to size or population. Most are like school projects or an expression of one's talent or ego. Others form when the creators buy land or an island, which is the most favorite type, and declare it a Country.

In this book are Laws & Government Codes, organized religion, History, Maps, USA/UEIR comparison, Mythology, Economy, Tax Codes, future projects, and other data. The requirements for becoming a Pharaoh are also included. Copyright © ® 2017 Pharaoh Horus Michael M7, All rights reserved.

© Pharaoh Horus Michael 1, Kingdom of Niihau

<u>**Note:**</u>

<u>**Fines for the Kingdom of Ni'ihau:**</u>

(In US$D Dollars or .999 Pure Silver):

1. Citation = $10, up to $100. If violator cannot pay or is disabled, violator may be assigned to Shabty Status.
2. Minor Fine = $100 up to $1000.
3. Major Fine = $250 to $10,000 or 15% of damages pertaining to crime committed.
4. Fines may be paid the same as Taxes.
5. Fine Revenue goes to State Treasury.
6. Fine Revenue *may also go to* local communities, Food Banks, Homeless Shelters, Disaster Relief, or to offset Tourism, Security, Intelligence, Farms, Fishing, or Natives of Niihau and other islands.
7. The Elder Council collects and sets price of Fines for violations, in Silver, US$, or Kahelelani shells.
8. Fines are recorded on file for all participants, Citizen, Plebe, etc.
9. Community Service is an alternative to paying Fines.

Appendix 1:

Legal Terms of Code Ma'at

Stealing:

Armed Robbery = To take items not owned by you, by forceful means such as with a weapon.

Normal, Unarmed Robbery = To take items not owned by you without permission such as from a Store or Marketplace.

Theft of items = To take objects from another person, place, or possession that are not yours, without permission.

Theft of Valuables = To take any item of value, such as Niihau Kahelelani Shell Leis, from a person or store, etc.

Theft of Food in a Store = To take food such as packaged bread, cookies, fruits, rice, etc. from a Store *without compensation* or payment to that Store.

Shoplifting = to take items from a Store without compensation or payment.

Major Shoplifting = to take highly valuable items from a Store, such as Technology or Jewelry without compensation.

Copyright © Infringement = to take written texts from a book or author and use it without compensation to that author or publishing company or permission, that say "Copyright © (Author name + year of registration)." This is not limited to books alone; photos, computer texts or programs, music, etc. are also valid. Copyright Protection is part of Government.

Plagiarism (unpaid, Cultural) = to steal ideas from another culture deliberately or without permission.

Plagiarism (paid) = to pay someone to steal ideas or to use ideas in a project for payment; stolen ideas can be trade secrets, imagination, creativity, inventions, novels, music, product ideas, company website ideas, etc.

Mugging on a public street = To capture a person in public (outside a building) and rob property from them.

Kidnapping (people) = to take people from their families for a duration of time, such as children or celebrities.

Kidnapping (animals) = to take animals from their homes for a duration of time.

Computer or Internet Theft = to take computers and other Technology without compensation of owners.

File sharing (paid) = to publicly distribute information such as bootlegged music or contraband or stolen books on technology (the Internet), for payment.

In Computer Game (Online) = to steal items from another user on an Internet game or program, without their permission.

Embezzlement (paid) = to acquire other peoples' money or payments entrusted to you such as investments, without their knowledge or permission.

Conspiracy to Steal = to plot or scheme or plan an action involving the act of Stealing.

Patent Theft = To steal items secured by a Patent or to steal ideas from a Patented item.

Piracy (real or online) = to take information from a published work for personal or paid usage, or to steal property using the Internet or other technology; also refers to Pirates on the open Seas.

Computer Hacking = to attack a website so as to acknowledge its faults for personal gain, such as vandalism or causing destruction of intellectual property.   Also refers to taking over websites away from actual owner.

Stealing personal data (Identity Theft) = to take information and use it maliciously or to assume the identity of someone else.

Data Mining or Phishing = to research information on a person or company for malicious intent, as with Identity Theft or Stalking. Also refers to tricking people into unlawfully giving you their personal information for criminal ends.

Crookedness = being corrupt in public or private, to commit crimes against people or society, to express evil or negative or hostile intentions.

Price Gouging & Petty Theft = to set prices in the markets that do not reflect actual value; to steal items of minor value.

Market Manipulation = to control prices in an economy for personal gain.

Deceptive Advertising = false description of a product, as with saying an object is an "Ancient Artifact" and charging a high price for it when in fact it is a tourist souvenir.

Deceiving Elderly or Disabled = to give false impression of a person, product or service for elderly and disabled people who cannot know the difference.

Obtaining Classified Data = stealing information that is classified top secret, confidential, or other classification from a Government.

Other Computer Theft = stealing computers, parts, or technology.

Computer Viruses (use) = using computer programs to disable or attack a website or computer belonging to someone else.

Key loggers = using a program that records patterns of keyboard commands for stealing passwords or credit card data or other data.

Key Duplication (non-owner) = to make a new key from a mold of an original for purpose of theft.

Cloning (non-medical) = to clone or copy an animal or person with Genetics for non-medical reasons, except for children.

Conquering (non-UEIR) = to take possession of a country or group by force, by Military, or by coup, that is not by the UEIR.

From Temples, Churches = to take items from a place of worship.

From Education Facilities = to steal from a school or College.

From States = to steal from a State or Country.

From Pharaoh = to steal from Pharaoh or Kings.

False Advertising = to give a false impression of a quality of a product for personal gain or a higher set value.

Mail Fraud = the act of falsely advertising a product via the postal service (mail order catalogs).

False Business = operating an organized crime business, or a business with no factual existence. *This excludes Micro-nations.*

Con Artistry (paid) = to operate an organized crime group or person for payment, to deceive for money purposes.

Entrapment = to snare a person or group into a situation they cannot escape from as with contracts or lies or other falsehood.

Eavesdropping (non-personal) = to listen to another's conversation for a public figure or person; to record conversations of a political office or person.

Wire-tapping (Personal) = to record maliciously any conversation on technology or cell phones.

Espionage (non-UEIR) = to spy on someone for collecting information or knowledge, of personal or of government or company secrets.

Agricultural Theft = to steal plants, seeds, bulbs, roots, flowers, nuts, etc. from a vegetation area for purposes of illegal transport into or out of a country or region.

Artifact Theft = to steal human-made objects or other cultural objects from a region, and for personal gain or collection (non Museum).

Hoarding (paid) = to be paid to hoard or store items *such as* flooding a market with currency to lower its value.

Photocopying (non-personal) = to copy papers or texts with technology that are Copyright © ® Protected.

Forgery of Currency = to replicate unlawfully a country's medium of exchange for use in trade *as if* it is the actual currency itself.

Forgery of Artifacts = to replicate unlawfully a cultural object to make it appear legitimate.

Forgery of UEIR Government = to replicate unlawfully anything of the UEIR.

False Claims = to falsely represent one's self for identity, honor, virtue, or position; to impart a deceptive belief about one's self to others.

False Inheritance Claims = to lie about one's relationship to claim an inheritance.

False Charity = to misrepresent one's self or business as a Charity; to collect funds as a charity without actually being one.

Unofficial Marketing = to advertise a product or service that is not in line with the actual company who makes it.

Grand Theft = to steal items of great value, such as an automobile, jewels, technology, trade secrets, or priceless artifacts.

Hidden Fees = unannounced surcharges or fees by a company that is not listed in the contract.

Immoral Company TOS = Terms of Service that violate laws of a State or Region, including sacred laws in religion or civil behavior (Maat).

Waiving Personal Rights = a practice of a company contract that removes Civil Rights via the contract obligations.

Undisclosed Fees = The same as Hidden Fees, except not disclosed or made public.

Lead coins (not gold) = using lead in place of gold for currency (same weight).

Killing:

Abortion (multiple, Late Term) = killing an unborn fetus right before birth or partial birth; or having many abortions in place of contraceptives.

Abortion (inconvenience) = having an abortion or killing an unborn fetus because you didn't want children or give birth to one, when you could have taken contraceptive medicine or practiced "safe sex."

Abortion (non-genetic defect) = *Abortions are legal in the UEIR* provided the reason is agreeable to the State. Such reasons include: genetic defect that causes life-threatening health conditions, injury to Mother, or injury to other children in the womb.

Premeditated, Multiple (serial killer) = thinking about killing someone then acting on this impulse, with intent to kill several others.

Mass Murder, Genocide = killing scores of people or their ethnicity.

Murder-Suicide = killing someone then killing yourself because you know it will result in your execution by the State.

Attempted M-S = trying to commit Murder-Suicide.

Terrorism with Murder = scaring people and killing them too.

Terrorism with malice = maliciously scaring people by destruction of property or explosions.

Terrorism with destruction = destroying property and scaring people. Terrorism is defined as the act of causing fear on a massive scale on a population for political or religious ideology or Movements.

Assault with weapons = attacking someone with a knife, gun, bomb, rock, or other instrument for purpose of injury.

Assault with intent to kill = attacking someone and wanting them dead from it.

Unintentional Assault = accidentally attacking someone, such as throwing a rock that hit a person by accident.

Accidental assault with weapon = discharging a gun without knowing it was loaded.

Accidental Assault = attacking someone with no intent to cause injury.

Accidental Killing = killing someone with no intent to kill.

Driving with Intent = collision into people while driving a vehicle.

Driving, accidental death = killing with a car with no intent to cause injury.

Driving with distraction = causing injury or death when distracted by non-driving actions such as music, texting, cell phones, etc.

DUI = *Driving under the Influence* = operating a vehicle while on drugs, alcohol, sex, or other distractions.

Cannibalism (Human) = eating Human flesh.

Sports Killing (Endangered Species) = hunting animals (etc.) that are rare in the wild or limited in population.

Hunting (non-food/Niihau) = hunting for sport without consumption or as food.

Technology Abuse (Animals) = testing medicine on animals for non medical reasons.

Chemical use (on people) = using abrasive chemicals on living people.

Killing with WMD = Weapons of Mass Destruction are illegal in the UEIR.

Nuclear War = using atomic weapons in a battle or war.

Deity Impersonation = pretending to be God(s) and then killing people who disagree with you.

Rioting = causing a large gathering of people (riot) who vandalize or destroy property.

Military Incursion = killing via an invading Army.

Protesting (armed) = rioters with weapons.

Protesting (peaceful) = rioters without weapons, but clog public streets and refuse to leave.

Subversion = undermining Civilization by recruitment of the populace with counter intelligence or political unrest.

Peaceful Terrorism = causing fear of people without destruction.

Anarchy, supporting Hostility = trying to overthrow a government with violence.

Religious Terrorism = using religion as a weapon to cause fear (Islam, 2017).

Destruction of Property = causing damage.

Vandalism, effacement = destroying property by attacking with weapons, such as breaking windows with sticks or rocks; or signs with spray paint.

Destroying Monuments = attacking a holy site like Pyramids, Temples, obelisks, statues, or stone edifices.

Extremism with Violence = using religion or ideas in the far right view coupled with violence or hostility.

Paid Assassination = hiring someone to kill another person, such as a government ruler.

Assassination = killing a ruler or official.

Conspiracy to Kill = planning to kill someone.

Attempt to overthrow government = planning to regime change the ruler.

Killing Ecosystem = killing natural habitat with chemicals or pollution.

Medical testing abuse, Food procurement abuse (animals) = maliciously using Medicine tests on animals without care of the animals, or abuse for food manufacturing such as with treatment in captivity.

Animal Abuse = abusing or mistreating animals.

Human Abuse = abusing or mistreating people.

Elderly abuse & neglect = mistreating Senior Citizens, not caring for them properly.

Assisted Suicide = Not protecting people with Depression, causing drug overdose, or encouraging suicide by public comments on the Internet.

Suicide (as weapon) = Islamic Terrorists are an example of this. Using suicide to cause destruction is unlawful, as with self-detonating a bomb on a person entering a building.

Forced Suicide = except as punishment, compelling someone to kill her or himself.

Drug use = using drugs to kill someone.

Medical Malpractice = Medical corruption that results in death of a patient.

Dental Malpractice = Dental corruption that results in death of a patient.

Single Murder = killing one person (*except in self-defense*).

Manslaughter = unintended death.

Internet Hoax = misusing technology to cause a situation resulting in a death.

Killing Police or Government (UEIR) = killing members of the UEIR Government.

Poisoning = administering a substance that results in death, such as chemicals, wild mushrooms, overdose of drugs, raw food, or certain plants.

Causing Diseases = carrying an illness in one's body that others are not immune to.

Deception:

Lying under oath = not telling the truth when sworn to do so under oath, as in a Court.

Lying to God(s) = not telling the truth to Akua.

Deceptive Behavior = actions that deceive.

Forged Documents = falsely creating documents that resemble real ones.

Deception of TOS = using Terms of Service to deceive intentions of company.

Un-disclosure of Facts = not giving facts correctly.

Industrial Espionage = spying on another company to steal trade secrets or product ideas.

Corruption (Bribery, extortion) = paying someone in Government for information about your neighbor, etc. This also means trying to gain money by extortion, threats, lawsuits, etc. Corruption can also show a lack of morality.

Greed, envy, wrath, sloth, lust, etc. (The Seven Deadly Sins) = greed – to over compensate one's self. Envy = to want another's property. Sloth = to be lazy. Wrath = enraged emotion. Lust = to want a relationship while married.

Deliberate Stupidity = to behave in a childish or unintelligent manner to escape Justice (*Obstruction of Justice*).

Bringing False Witnesses (in Court) = lying to cover up a crime, by saying what didn't happen in an event.

False Pedigree, Education = a false College Degree or honor, rank, etc.

Dressing as UEIR = wearing UEIR Official outfits so as to misrepresent your identity.

False Imprisonment = foreign police who arrest or imprison a UEIR agent, officer, official or citizen.

False inheritance = a false claim of inherited property.

Political Incorrectness = not behaving in a civil fashion in view of other Nations.

Immoral Gossip = spreading rumors or information that is not factual, or based on opinions, without contacting the subject directly.

Slander or Libel = written or verbal comments that attack a person's fame, credibility, honor, valor, virtue, or self-esteem. *Low ratings on a product will do this.*

Malicious Rumors = hostile falsehoods about a subject spread by mass media or cell phones.

Deceptive Terrorism = using terrorism to deceive a region with *Fake News*.

Disrespect = attacking one's honor with insults.

Destruction:

Assault = to attack with force, as by hitting, kicking, biting, pummeling, ramming, etc.

General Violence = showing hostility in the public, or assaulting, rioting, or subversion.

Vandalism, Graffiti = destroying or damaging property by writing names on walls or windows, by setting fires or breaking objects like signposts, fire hydrants, windows, monuments, gravesites, statues, idols, etc.

Illegal Fireworks = using pyrotechnics that are forbidden by Law due to wildfires probability or likely injury.

IED Device = Improvised Explosive Device, a bomb or other incendiary.

Booby-trap = a snare or net that is laid out to trap someone or something, like an animal.

Biological Weapons = use of contained diseases, viruses, Genetic Material, bacteria for use as a weapon to kill or cause an epidemic.

Chemical Weapons = use of chemicals to cause destruction or kill people.

Psychic Weapons = weaponized Psychic Abilities, such as Telekinesis or Elemental.

War Crimes = crimes occurring in a War that is disagreed by most Nations, such as Genocide, using Chemical, Biological, or Nuclear Weapons, or subversion of a population. Crimes against Humanity are a common form.

Crimes against Gods, Earth, Humanity, Nature = War Crimes on a particular subject; anything harming religious artifacts, widespread pollution, against Human Nature or people, and the Environment.

Infrastructure Damage = destroying bridges, roads, airports, etc.

Torture (non-UEIR) = abuse of living people to acquire information or as punishment for a crime.

Cruelty towards Life (etc.) = negative abuse of living people.

Psychic Feedback (Telepsi) = attacking the voice heard by millions of people in the psychic realm (**M7**).

Occult Wars = wars occurring with Magic Spells, curses, etc.

Trojans, Hacking Programs = programs that enter a computer as if beneficial then attack it, via the Internet.

Cyber Wars, Terrorism = misuse of the Internet Technology to conduct unlawful attacks against websites and connected devices or companies.

Car-hijacking = taking an automobile by using parts of it, such as wires.

Disturbing the Peace = causing public disturbances like riots, assaults, vulgarity, insults, or other actions.

Bullying = to abuse children with strength or threats of force.

Retaliation, blackmail, threats = to counter attack an enemy in public, issuing written notices to intimidate them, or unlawful use of force.

Revenge Destruction = to cause property damage in a counter attack to an enemy.

Sex Crimes:

Rape = non permitted sexual penetration by either gender, or the pillaging of a country during war.

Harassment = repeated comments that are of a sexual or other undesired subject matter.

Sexual Assault = attack on one's sex organs, body parts, or intention of undesired reproductive acts.

Incest = the act of sex with one's ethnicity or distant family member (*except 3ʳᵈ cousins*), such as a brother/sister.

Polygamy = having multiple wives or husbands in a relationship.

Promoting Gender bias = supporting false information based on gender.

Promoting Bisexuality, etc. = supporting the idea of having sex with both genders at the same time or with same person (M/M/F or F/F/M not M/F only).

Relationships:

Political Marriage = a false union of countries.

Marriage for Profit = marriage that is for making money in divorces, such as marrying a rich person and quickly divorcing him/her for profit.

Hate Crimes = violence attributed to Hate Groups such as racial, ethnic, sexual or religious.

Harassment by Media = photographers who endanger their subjects by reckless driving, repeated actions, violence, or intrusion.

Stalking = the act of following, intimidating, spying on, wearing clothing from, or invading the privacy of any person as with perceived but not realized relationships.

Public Disturbance = causing loud noises at night when people are sleeping, or being **drunk in public or in disorderly conduct**.

Religious Laws:

Heresy or Blasphemy = saying falsehoods or insults against a religious figure, Deity, Priest, Prophet, Christ, Pharaoh, Akua, or other entity.

Imposing *Sharia Laws* on Niihau = using Islamic religious laws on the islands.

Burning "Marijuana Incense" = use of incense flavored or scented with the drug.

Praying against the Akua = use of Magic or Prayers to attack the Akua or Gods.

Willing people to death = use of prayer to kill.

Touching body of Akua = Do not touch the Akua! They are sacred.

<u>**Notes:**</u>

The **Islands** mentioned in this book were legally purchased **via the USA Government** on behalf of **Pharaoh M7.**

Niihau was purchased from Helen Robinson on July 5, 2000 (she died in 2002) for $2B; it was valued at $500M. The island was being planned to be sold anyway due to debts, until the Military leased their base.

Lanai was purchased on October 29, 2015 for $12B (from Oracle CEO, Larry Ellison, whom originally paid $400M. The islanders refused to cooperate with his designs for money-making ideas, such as a Wealthy-only camping resort, Desalination for water, etc.).

Kahoolawe was sold on December 6, 2016 for $26M. It is on reserve for a "Native Hawaiian Government."

Molokai was *said to be purchased* on August 7, 2017 (***Pending***) for $16B.   Pharaoh M7 has only visited **Molokai** once. **Niihau is a "Native Hawaiian Reservation"** Island, also called *The Forbidden Island.*

The Well-Traveled Adze

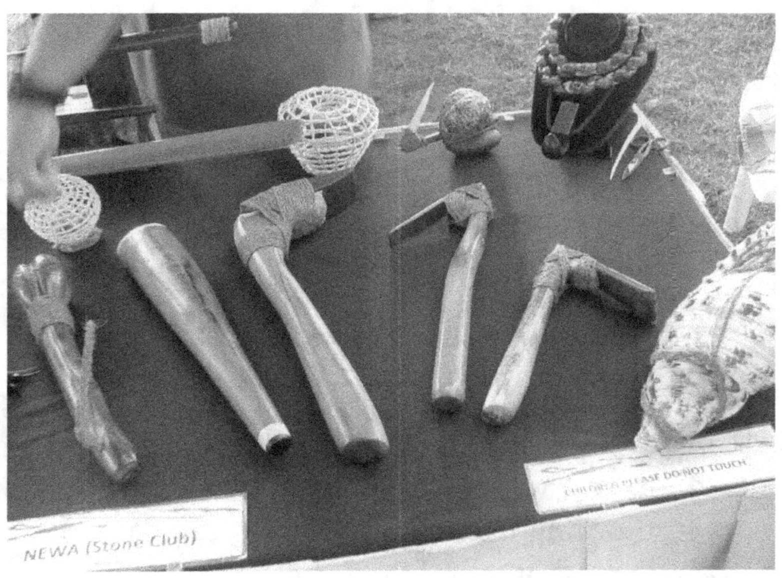

The origins of Ancient Hawaii may be attributed to Ancient Egypt's last heirs. **It is widely believed by Archaeologists** that Civilization with no Trade Routes evolved on their own, independent of each other, containing the exact same ideas, beliefs and technology. **This is somewhat wrong.** By the invasion of the Romans in 30 BCE, some Egyptians boarded ships and left the Mediterranean and arrived in the New World via the seas between Africa and South America. They **migrated to Peru and later Central America**, founding the Inca and Toltecs, Mayans, and Olmec cultures. On the way from the New World they **migrated to Polynesia**, and later **Hawaii.**

<u>Ideas brought from Egypt to Hawaii:</u>

1. Petroglyphs (Picture Writing; Hieroglyphs).
2. Use of Feathers in costume.
3. Unification of Islands by conquest.
4. The Carpenter's Adze tool.
5. Stone-built Temples.
6. Natural Polytheism & Energy Magic.
7. Underground Tombs (Kamehameha tomb).
8. Travel by boat.
9. Mortar and Pestle (Stone tools).
10. Stone or wooden Statues (Tiki).
11. Offerings to the Gods (necklace, Leis).
12. Kings and Chieftains (Alii; Nomarch).
13. Basket Weaving (Reed mats).
14. Clothing from plants (Bark Cloth, Linen).
15. Laws (Kapu System; Ma'at).

The **Inca Emperor** believed the same as the Egyptian Pharaoh in that "Everything below the Sun belongs to him." They also practiced **mummification** by natural drying of the skin on high mountains. **Ideas are considered artifacts**. The Aztecs (Toltecs) had Sun Pyramids and worshiped the Sun and Moon, had human sacrifice, Jaguar skins, hieroglyphs, Polytheism, and honored a "Man from the East who gave them civilization" called **Quetzalcoatl** (**Osiris**) who promised to return in the Future (**M7**).

In 2008 I participated in a Genetic Study by the **National Geographic Society**, using Genetic material from my Y-Chromosome. It contained "North Africa & the Middle East" genes.

It also contained **DNA from Polynesia**. My paternal family [Costa] is currently Portuguese from **Madeira Islands**, formerly called *Atlantis* (*past the Pillars of Hercules into the Atlantic Ocean*). My family was originally from Ancient Egypt and migrated to Portugal. They remained in Portugal after the Inquisition there, where ancestry of Semitic origins was forced to be Catholic Christian or return home. My paternal family is Catholic with Semitic names (Hebrew names). The location of this family originates in Egypt. The family was **Plantation Owners** in colonial Hawaii. They later moved to California in USA. The family migrated to Hawaii, bringing the *Ukulele* (Musical Instrument) with them. Whenever I visit Hawaii, *Mana Energy* resonates within me. This is the power of the **Akua** - supernatural people who lived with Ancient Hawaiians and were venerated by them. **As an Akua**, I am attempting to unite these Hawaiian Islands for a Native Hawaiian Kingdom, as desired by anyone presently living in Hawaii who resented the confiscation of the islands by *"American Businessmen who dissolved the Hawaiian Monarchy"* in making Hawaii a State in USA.

The **Adze** was the **tool** used in the Egyptian *Opening of the Mouth Ceremony* (Last Rites, similar to Christian Communion). It was held by the **KheriHeb Priest**, and enabled the soul to use its abilities again after death and into rebirth. The **Adze** is shaped like a "**7**."

The following **ideas** from the **UEIR** were publicly advertised by the USA since 1993:

1. Ionic Pillars, Egyptian symbols
2. Egyptian ruler with Fez cap and handlebar moustache
3. The words "**Flawed**" (*The Flawed Emerald*, also called *Eye of the Pharaoh* ©1990, 1995 MJC); "**Hero**" (from Plebeian Law Code ©1996 UEIR); "**Legacy**" (Code Caesar 1999); "**Inner Circle**" (UEIR laws); "**Imperial Republic**"; "**American Pharaoh**"; etc.
4. Partial Caduceus (S7).
5. M7 (from *you-know-who*).
6. Black, White, Red colors (Egyptian flag).
7. Inverted Text (black/white box of name)
8. Yin-Yang / Emotes / ☺ / Hieroglyphs
9. Anything about Julius Caesar (S7) or Egypt
10. "Revenge is Justice" (Barternote Currency)

The marketing is for UEIR Citizens to recognize and unite as a Country; the majority already did react in the mid 1990s with the distribution of *Eye of the Pharaoh* novel by MC. This is evidence of recognition.

www.amazon.com/author/horusmichael

www.amazon.com/author/michaeljcosta